Stephan Scholtissek

Innovation Excellence

Stephan Scholtissek

Innovation Excellence

Creating Market Success in the Energy
and Natural Resources Sector

This book was developed as part of the research programme at the Accenture Innovation Centre for Energy and Utilities. The centre is a research and innovation hub developed to bring innovation, thought leadership and insight to the topics of policy, consumers, sustainability, technology and industry transition within the context of the energy and utility industry landscape.
For more information, visit www.accenture.com/innovation-center.

Bibliographic information from the Deutsche Nationalbibliothek
Die Deutsche Nationalbibliothek registers this publication in the Deutsche Nationalbibliografie. Detailed bibliographic information can be retrieved at http://dnb.d-nb.de

British Library Cataloguing-in-Publication Data
A CIP record for this book is available from the British Library.

Library of Congress Cataloging-in-Publication Data
A CIP record for this book is available from the Library of Congress.

First published in Germany in 2011 by mi-Wirtschaftsbuch, an imprint of FinanzBuch Verlag GmbH, Munich, Germany, as "Innovation Excellence: Creating Market Success in the Energy and Natural Resources Sector" by Stephan Scholtissek. All rights reserved.

© 2011 by mi-Wirtschaftsbuch, FinanzBuch Verlag GmbH
Nymphenburger Str. 86
D-80636 München, Germany
www.mi-wirtschaftsbuch.de

ISBN 978-3-86880-124-8

Edition Kogan Page 2011

Published and distributed in Great Britain, United States and India by Kogan Page Limited.

ISBN 978 0 7494 63465

120 Pentonville Road	1518 Walnut Street, Suite 1100	4737/23 Ansari Road
London N1 9JN	Philadelphia PA 19102	Daryaganj
United Kingdom	USA	New Delhi 110002
www.koganpage.com		India

Coverdesign by Jarzina Kommunikations-Design, Holzkirchen, Germany
Typeset by Julia Walch, Bad Soden
Illustrations page 17, 20, 28, 75 by iStockphoto.com; page 18, 109, 110 by Getty Images
Printed by Firmengruppe APPL, aprinta Druck, Wemding
Printed in Germany

Contents

Foreword

Time and time again in my 20 years as a management consultant, corporate executives have asked me the same two questions: "How can we grow without snapping up rivals?" and "How can we secure lasting success when competition is getting fiercer by the day?" These questions have lost none of their urgency, but since the implosion of the dot-com bubble and the sharpest recession in generations triggered by the credit crisis, I am also regularly asked a third: "What can I do to shield my business against similar earth-shattering events in the future?"

My answer to all three questions is the word that is at the very heart of this book: innovation. The word is powerful, I've found. It usually triggers lively discussions. "So, you recommend hiring more scientists?" top-level managers tend to respond. Or, "OK, then, please set up an innovation project for us lasting, say, three months." Or, in a clear indication that innovation is still widely seen as something purely for manufacturers, I also often hear, "Well, you know, we're into services here. We don't make products."

All these responses are evidence of widespread misunderstandings around what innovation is, how it comes about and how it should be conducted. Contrary to popular belief, it is not made in laboratories – a scientist's bright idea is always only as good as its commercial success. Innovation is not just for transitory use in a company. And of course it is certainly not something that can only be applied to physical products. You can bring about innovation by revamping what you market, your business model, your processes or even the organisation of your company. And in all these cases it does not just happen in dribs and drabs, here and there, only now and then. To become really effective, innovation must be deeply rooted in a business' DNA.

As a young biochemical scientist I was able to witness how inventions conceived in my native Germany often failed to bring economic benefit to their originators. This was either because bureaucracy stood in the way, society and politics had been slow to mobilise enthusiasm, or the companies themselves simply failed to spot the potential commercial merits of their own brainchildren – and competitors ran away with them.

I left the academic ivory tower with a PhD under my belt to join the corporate world, where I soon noticed that even blue-chip companies find it difficult to build a system that turns excellent ideas swiftly into revenue. To this day corporate entities are frequently held back by compartmentalised thinking, rigid legacy cultures or awkward silo structures. It is therefore hardly surprising that many lack a stringent innovation process: a suite of defined frameworks combined with driving minds free enough to propel good ideas uninhibited to market.

Cross-pollination is key to this. Imagine the following: young graduates applying to your company are asked at the job interview what they would like to do – marketing, research and development, production or sales. "All of that together!" replies one. If your human resources officer looks up and says, "Hired!" your business has caught the innovation bug and you have probably discovered a true innovation talent. But if the response is, "Sorry, you have to pick one," your business may have a way to go.

It was as a consultant that I was finally able to see innovation processes up close in real businesses. Over the years I have had the privilege of meeting numerous true innovators. They included shrewd owner-operators of family firms, visionary upstart entrepreneurs and clever minds embedded in huge corporate environments. Each of them had led a product or service to market success. Talking to and working closely with them allowed me to discover the views, rules, patterns, procedures and ultimate success factors that made up their approaches. This solidified into a clear set of stages and practical rules that could guide the building of a viable innovation process in any company.

All this know-how is packed into the compact book you hold in your hands. In it I analyse and structure the innovation process theoretically, then square it immediately with real examples of successful innovation in the energy and natural resources sector. This is not only an industry that has my natural attention as a trained biochemist, but one that, being extremely competitive globally, has come up with a series of truly remarkable innovations. It should make the book a particularly useful read for executives in the raw materials, energy, chemicals and utility industries as well as for industry association leaders and those who buy from or sell to these companies. However, the basic innovation principles described here are universal and can benefit your company no matter what sector you are in.

Acknowledgements

Much like a good innovation process, this book has been a team effort. Its development has involved numerous people from around the world coming together to achieve a common goal. They contributed through interviews, assessments of the innovation process and reviews of the manuscript. I would like to express my appreciation to each of them.

In particular, I would like to thank the following for sharing their valuable time and insights: Ewald Beinhardt, Wolfgang Dörmer, Jackie Fionda, Philip New and Patrick Wendeler (Aral and BP); Don Sheets, Shelley Bausch (Dow Corning); Dr. Alfred Oberholz, Dr. Peter Nagler (Evonik Degussa); Ignacio Sánchez Galán (Iberdrola); Kevin Bogard, Dave Hesher, Don McCord and Cheryl Miller (Marathon); Emmanuel Manichon (Nestlé Waters); Professor Udo Ungeheuer, Dr. Hans-Joachim Konz, Dr. Lutz Klippe, Dr. Friedrich Siebers (Schott); Barbara Kux, Dr. Reinhold Achatz, Andreas Hauser, Dr. Jochen Koelzer and John Lombardo (Siemens).

I owe a special debt of gratitude to those of my Accenture colleagues – Dr. Matthias Feistel, Felix Hessel and Wolfgang Popp – who helped with the development and refinement of the innovation framework and success factors, which form the very core of this book.

The text would also not be what it is without the excellent advice and help I have received from my editorial team – Ulf Henning, Laura Kopec, Matthew McGuinness and Jens Schadendorf. Warmest thanks to all of them.

Other Accenture colleagues I would like to thank include Mark Davisson, Bettina Igler, Ken Johnson, Colin Lowenberg, Valentín Miguel and Haralds Robeznieks.

I am also hugely grateful to my Munich-based publisher mi-Wirtschaftsbuch/FinanzBuch Verlag GmbH, in particular CEO Christian Jund and Editor

Michael Wurster for their extraordinary enthusiasm, professionalism and wonderfully quick and flexible handling of this project.

Finally, I would also like to thank Helen Kogan, head of Kogan Page, London, and her team, in particular Jon Finch, for their lively engagement and their industrious and adroit support in bringing this book to the global market.

Introduction

Innovation – the hunt for a gem in a new age of competition

Early economists asked a simple question: why is it that something as useful as water is available so cheaply whereas diamonds, with such limited practical use, are so expensive? The answer to this intriguing riddle was that water is widely available and diamonds are not. From this we derive a fundamental economic principle: it is the degree of scarcity that puts different price tags on different things.

The deeper dimensions of this idea are best left to academic lecture theatres. For the practical world of economic enterprises the principle sheds a useful light on vital business inputs such as labour, capital, land or ideas. Their scarcity, availability and affordability will change dramatically over the next twenty years when the balance of global economic power shifts further towards emerging countries, reflecting the trend towards globalisation.

Let's look at it like this: there is the old world that most of us are familiar with and the majority of enterprises still see themselves as being up against. Here, things like skilled workers, suitable factory sites, natural resources, access to funding, affordable energy or even the right customer groups are vital business ingredients and hard to come by. Our experience tells us that these ingredients are available to different degrees – and therefore today still command substantially different market prices – around the world. Hence, a software engineer in Bangalore is still paid a fraction of the wage his identically skilled colleague in Boston receives. And it is certainly still true today that getting hold of a hard-currency loan in Botswana is more difficult and expensive than it is in Berlin.

But this is the core point about the not too distant future: in the new world of global competition – the birth of which we are witnessing – the hunt for rare business factors, these diamonds of various quality, purity and value, will become much less important if not, at some point, insignificant. Labour, capital, knowledge and other inputs necessary to set up shop will adopt the quality of commodities and be available – almost like water – at more or less globally harmonised prices. That does not necessarily mean they will become more affordable, but their still widely differing market values will gravitate into a narrower band. When virtually everything is available to everyone at a similar price, businesses around the world will find themselves in pursuit of a last remaining precious gemstone – innovation. Unlike the other inputs, this factor, by definition, is always "rare" enough to command outstanding prices. A distinct product, an exclusive patent, a pioneering production process, distribution channel, supply-chain mechanism or brand promise – any of these could make the difference for a company. In the new age of hyper-competition, what will distinguish you in the eyes of customers, rivals and shareholders will simply be the quantity of successful innovations you can come up with. This all-important capacity will hinge on you having a viable innovation process in place and the consistency with which you can make it work for you.

You might think innovation is something relative. How can novelty be measured accurately? How good is a good idea or a clever invention? There is a surgically precise answer: a good invention is nothing unless it can prove itself to be a success in the market place. Numerous truly good ideas falter because of bad implementation on their way to market. And an equal number initially thought to be wonderful end as hopeless cases because, contrary to preliminary assumptions, they simply fail to strike a cord with customers. The Austrian-American economist Joseph A. Schumpeter put it in a nutshell back in 1911: "Innovation is the process of finding economic applications for inventions." This means it is only when an invention has been marketed successfully that we can call it an innovation. The yardstick is simple: new ideas are successful on the market when increased sales and decreased costs push the invention across the threshold of profitability.

We can get a clear, practical sense of innovation's power by looking to Germany. The country has only recently lost its status as the world's biggest export nation to China. Of course China has won the game (for now) by playing according to different rules: most of its products are still less sophisticated and manufactured with much lower labour costs. Germany, by contrast, was able for many decades to produce globally sought after export goods even with some of the world's highest labour costs. The feasibility of this approach came down to one thing: innovation. This factor alone kept and still keeps a large number of German products and services in the game worldwide and many of those are still way ahead of the competition.

Moreover, despite their success, German companies have hardly been the world's most active takeover buccaneers, which leads to another interesting point about innovation: having the capacity and knowledge to turn good ideas swiftly into huge commercial successes on the market will also eventually be

China has outmanoeuvered Germany as the biggest producer of solar panels

the last viable alternative to buying rivals or crowding them out by lowering prices. Both of the latter strategies, numerous studies have made clear, show only mixed long-term results in margin improvement or shareholder value enhancement. From that point of view, even today a buzzing innovation pipeline already makes for the healthiest way a company can stem competition and achieve sufficient growth. In that regard, innovation will definitely be your best protection in any rough weather the globalised era might have in store.

The global harmonisation of business input costs discussed above will probably happen in just a decade and a half or so – with innovation remaining the sole exception. In fact, Indian outsourcing firms concede already that an IT specialist in Boston will, in only a few years, rival their staff in Bangalore on pay. In this general equalisation trend, the knowledge market will explode in volume – particularly driven by the transparency the internet creates. Patents and trademarks, the powerful protectors of intellectual property, will be traded easily on a deep and liquid world market between Shenzen, Stuttgart and San Francisco. Globally harmonised patent laws will make concepts and inventions available to anybody who feels entrepreneurial and wants to set up a business. They will turn into a resource like, say, energy is today. Companies in this environment will need to ensure they do not fall between the cracks, wasting money on poorly conceived internal R&D, then being unable to compete as buyers in the innovation market. Quicker idea generation will also be decisive, as innovations lose value faster in this highly competitive environment. Remember, it took one million years for mankind to modernise the axe and develop metal knives. Today a computer mouse becomes technologically dated within just five years.

Innovation pioneer
Joseph A. Schumpeter

The scenario laid out here is a multi-polar world. It will unfold at many economic epicentres and various poles of corporate power scattered around the globe. Whoever has deep enough pockets will be able to set up shop anywhere in no time and create difficulties for an established blue-chip company even on its home turf. We see plenty of early evidence of this already. Over the past decade, China, India, Russia and Brazil have turned up the heat on the USA, Western Europe and Japan – the economic establishment of the last century. Yes, the latter three regions are still the predominant well of technological and scientific innovation. Yet just a few recent headlines indicate the tectonic shift that is underway. Brazil has overtaken Germany as the world's fourth largest car market. Russia has launched commercial passenger jets to rival an established duopoly of Western manufacturers. The same is true of China, an economic powerhouse that has already outmanoeuvred Germany as the biggest producer of solar panels and recently registered the most worldwide patents in a year. India, meanwhile, has come up with the most affordable mass car ever developed, while South Korea's universities churn out more engineers every academic year in absolute numbers than the United States.

In a striking additional development, more and more world-class executives and managers are crossing the lines to head ambitious corporate organisations in emerging countries. In doing so, they are transferring the leadership skills and innovation experience they have garnered in the mature markets of the West to new hotspots in fast growing markets. Even this segment of the labour market is turning global as pay packages for international talent begin to harmonise.

In the energy and natural resources industries the new world has already knocked at the door

Why are the historic shifts described above especially vital to the energy and natural resources industries, our main focus in this book? Put simply, there is less time left in this sector before these changes begin to bite. In many respects the markets for these industries – raw material groups, power producers, oil and gas companies and chemicals manufacturers – are undergoing massive change as the balance of power shifts towards emerging economies and the world looks to a range of low carbon technologies.

With the economic boom propelling emerging countries like China, India and Brazil, markets have become tight for most companies in the energy and natural resources sector as the global run to secure deposits of oil, gas, uranium and fertilisers reaches new heights. In one of a string of similar deals, the state oil company Petroleos de Venezuela (PDVSA) and China National Petroleum Corporation agreed to extract and refine 2.9 billion barrels of crude oil annually in Eastern Venezuela over a 25-year period. Chinese energy companies are also desperate to secure energy supplies in the Middle East, West-Africa and Central Asia for the country's rapidly growing economy.

Many other state-owned emerging world energy companies have entered the race. In the oil sector, for instance, they are increasingly pushing the big diversified Western oil majors into new territory where innovation is becoming vital. As oil producing countries go for the easy oil and gas in their own ground, Western exploration expertise is increasingly left with technologically ambitious, costly and risky projects such as deepwater drilling, oil sand or shale gas.

For the moment the raw materials sector is enjoying the second super-cycle since the turn of the century. Spot prices for everything from industrial metals to rare earths, coke and coal are booming, largely driven by the voracious appetites of countries like China, India and Indonesia that have a relative dearth of rich deposits in their own soil. Dividends and returns for shareholders in the sector have never been higher. The success of raw material companies is actually almost too much for them. Bottlenecks arise in the shape of transport capacity limits, a difficulty that nevertheless looks like a nice problem to have from the perspective of other sectors facing stubborn structural growth problems.

But the current all-singing-all-dancing commodity party is also deceptive. Once the froth is gone and the rush has decelerated to more normal speeds, growing a company in this sector – whether in mature or emerging markets – will be a lot more difficult. Many areas within the mining, oil or energy sectors are already highly consolidated. For instance, three quarters of the world's shipped iron ore – the most important raw material for steel production and the bedrock of industrial development – is now provided, subsequent to fierce consolidation rounds, by just three dominant suppliers. Buying a rival to grow is an idea that might quickly be shot down now anyway by industry regulators or hidden government agendas. Canada has just blocked the foreign takeover of its fertiliser champion Potash, which controls a third of the global market. Takeover opportunities in the sector have become minimal for the top players. The alternative – waiting for the next super-cycle to emerge – could be too much of a drag financially and a difficult sell to shareholders.

This is where a well oiled innovation process can save the day, giving businesses real differentiation as a route to growth.

Interestingly, in some quarters, the energy and natural resources sector still has an unjustified reputation for being less than dynamic in its approach to innovation. Its activities are often only associated with dirty oil-men on rigs or dusty miners underground. In energy production an image prevails of a distinctly utilitarian utilities sector where customers – retail and corporate – respond not to shrewdly innovative propositions, but to a sheer, basic need for gas, water or electricity.

And indeed, on the surface, this sector's spending for research and development seems to be modest, as the average share rarely exceeds three percent of annual sales. On the other hand, it relies heavily on business-to-business relationships and therefore, by nature, leans more towards innovation in processes, services or business models than physical products. This kind of innovation activity is rarely reflected in officially published R&D spending figures.

Our research into this sector's innovations duly went much deeper than such figures. As this book will demonstrate, the perception of the sector as a dull laggard is a caricature. Of particular interest is the finding that environmental sustainability and green technology are particulary high on innovation agendas here.

We will profile eight well known companies that have shown a remarkable capacity to innovate: BP, Dow Corning, Evonik Industries, Iberdrola, Marathon, Perrier, Schott and Siemens. They have achieved innovations in products, business models, services, marketing, processes and organisations – leading to measurable market success.

Each of them went through – or at least came close to – a stringent and complete six-stage innovation process, from a clear initial mechanism of idea finding through systematic planning and evaluation phases, creation of a business case and running of a piloting stage to, finally, successful market entry and rapid expansion. We outline this process in detail in the Innovation Process chapter.

Additionally, we will cover several inventions that show great promise for market success in the near future – from smart grids, predictive maintenance, biofuels and geothermal energy, to solar shingles, wireless electricity, travelling wave nuclear reactors, and concentrated solar thermal power plants.

Innovation – ultimately the boardroom holds the reins

What is true for the energy and natural resources sector is broadly valid for any business: a thoroughly implemented innovation process can plant the all-important innovation mode deep enough in a company to make it its normal way of thinking. This book's case studies will analyse success factors to illustrate that innovation management is primarily the duty of the chief executive officer – and always his or her finest hour.

It is only the company head who can bear the responsibility and risk that go with decisions taken during a rigorous innovation project. Certainly the individual steps in the process are normally planned and taken by a dedicated team or another innovator authority within the company such as an inventor or an expert scientist. But, like it or not, only the CEO's power can shield new ideas from rivalry, inertia and skepticism in the rest of the company – and this is what unprecedented thinking will inevitably face in an established, large corporate environment. Innovations are by nature "creative destroyers" – the more comprehensive they are, the greater their revolutionary power to create something truly new. In that regard innovations are trouble makers, and they are meant to be. But that is precisely why they should not be locked away in secluded satellite incubators but rather pushed centre-stage in a business – and that is something that only top level management has the authority to do.

As our case studies will show, steering innovation through the boardroom is also essential. A visionary idea, once singled out for development, will at some stage need the support of the company as a whole. In particular, when a clever product or service has left the drawing board to be pushed to market, it will likely require the unreserved dedication, energy and momentum of marketing, logistics and sales.

Leadership power at the top also ensures that boundaries can be blurred – they often need to be torn down completely – between established core business and innovative areas. Having the innovator authority right at the helm is the easiest way to encourage the whole organisation to think and act along the kind of flexible, open-minded lines usually seen at start-up firms. With proper innovation-minded leadership you can effortlessly move even a big beast in your industry along quick tactical and strategic gambits.

Small-scale attackers like start-ups cannot be a threat in the innovation arena to incumbents with all their research capability, funding power and staff-skills – as long as the latter preserve a start-up spirit and base innovation development on seed investments and a diverse portfolio of projects. With this in place, even the largest corporate organism can start to run entirely on an incessant stream of innovative thinking. This is a major responsibility for management, but it ensures that new ideas flow freely and have a chance to prove their commercial clout.

Types
of Innovation

Product, service, organisational, process, business model, and marketing

The greater part of modern economic history, covering roughly the last 200 years, is associated with groundbreaking tangible inventions spawned by rapidly progressing knowledge in science and engineering. Translated into runaway successes when brought to market, they mark an era of highly visible innovations. However, this focus on products tends to obscure the fact that innovation has other, less tangible, but nevertheless important aspects: the way a business is run, how company processes are plugged into one another, how sales channels are organised and corporate cultures defined. In many industries, innovation in these areas can be much more important for profits and losses than isolated zingy ideas dreamed up by traditional research and development teams. Let's, therefore, briefly run through a contemporary typology of innovation types before examining specific examples of successful innovation.

Product Innovation

Products, of course, represent the most obvious type of innovation. The personal computer or the MP3 player, electrically powered watches, the wall plug, the power drill or baking soda – all these innovations caused smaller or larger revolutions in their respective domains. Compared to the electric typewriter, which was the standard in the 1980s, the personal computer represented a giant technological leap. The same goes for the MP3 player compared to the CD player or the automobile compared to the horse-drawn carriage.

Product innovations can be entirely new products, new designs or technologies applied to existing products or new applications of existing products. Mere advancements or refinements of existing products, however, are not innovations.

Service Innovation

Services that are able to satisfy customer needs in new ways also represent innovations. They can be entirely new services themselves or major improvements to existing ones. The new element might be the time of day at which the service is provided, the service provider or a billing model, to name a few examples.

Organisational Innovation

An organisational innovation involves division of labour – responsibilities and roles within a business – being modified or restructured. This allows the company to reposition itself in the market, increase flexibility and improve internal processes. German specialty chemicals supplier Evonik, which we will look at in an upcoming chapter, is a striking example of this. The company has created extremely fluid organisational set-ups for its different departments and divisions, allowing it to bring new product ideas to fruition extremely quickly.

Process Innovation

Process innovations involve new or adapted processes that link different factors and activities. They are introduced in order to create new products or services or to make production of existing products and delivery of existing services faster, better quality or cheaper.

Probably the most famous ever process innovation was the introduction of mass production for Ford's Tin Lizzy motor car model in 1908. Here the innovation was not the engine, transmission or chassis, but the manufacturing process itself. The assembly line dramatically reduced production time and cost and was the birth of industrial mass production.

Business Model Innovation

Until a few years ago, if you wanted to buy a book, you had to visit your local bookshop. Today, you have the entire world of books at your fingertips through your PC thanks to virtual bookshops such as Amazon. In a similar vein, you

Marketing Innovation

used to have to browse the classifieds or make a trip to your local flea market to buy or sell secondhand items – until the arrival of eBay, the first online auction house. Amazon and eBay are two examples of innovative business models.

A business model innovation is a new or modified combination of business strategy, technology, structure and processes. Together, these components create a business model that can make a company stand out from its competitors, ideally creating a unique position in the market. An aspect that is often neglected in the invention of new business models is division of labour. It was economic specialisation that allowed Amazon to achieve market success quickly. The online trader focused on sales and marketing while delegating logistics to partner businesses.

Marketing Innovation

To my mind, the best definition of a marketing innovation comes from the Centre for European Economic Research (ZEW) in Mannheim, Germany: "A marketing innovation is the implementation of a new marketing method that the company has previously not employed. Marketing innovations are part of a new marketing concept or a new marketing strategy involving significant changes in product and/or service design, packaging, product placement, distribution channels, product promotion or pricing."

This exhaustive attempt nevertheless falls down on two points. First, it claims that a marketing innovation – and by implication probably any innovation – does not always include novelty. Yet a company that copies a competitor's innovation is not in itself innovating, only imitating or adapting. Secondly, the definition fails to include market success. Without it, any unconventional marketing campaign would be "innovative" even if the marketed product turned out to be a shelf warmer.

An example of innovative power is the marketing of the Jägermeister brand: through event and viral marketing, the brand with the sign of the stag does not so much sell a herbal liqueur as a licence to push back the boundaries of common decency.

Hybrids

From the many success stories in this book, we can identify a trend: innovations are increasingly combining different innovation types.

Although we rarely think about it, countless things that make our life more convenient already fall into this category. The cashpoint machine or ATM was a groundbreaking product innovation and, at the same time, an innovative service that meant bank customers no longer had to stand in line at the counter to withdraw cash. Similar examples are legion – for instance, the "all-in-one chip" for low-budget mobile phones introduced by Infineon in 2007: an innovative product with a profound process innovation behind it. Another example is the emergency medical service Stroke Angels, an innovative service based on a highly complex process innovation. It allows paramedics caring for a suspected stroke patient to collect medical data quickly via an electronic note pad that radios the information straight to the emergency room.

A truly extraordinary example is the fashion chain Zara, which combines nearly all the innovation types described here. This is why Daniel Piette, fashion director at Louis Vuitton, called Zara "… possibly the most innovative and devastating retailer in the world" – and rightly so. Innovations are "creative destroyers," the more so the more comprehensive they are.

BP:
Aral Ultimate Diesel

01

Eleven workstreams fuelling one idea: a new petrol

Among the dozens of gloomy warehouses lying idle in Hattingen, an old German coal town in the Ruhr area, one, for a while, harbours an almost surreal scene: a brand new petrol station, illuminated by glaring blue and white light, the corporate colours of BP's German petrol brand Aral. The British oil giant has made this unlikely place, nicknamed Pump Clinic, the test-bed for one of the most ambitious oil industry product innovations in years: Aral Ultimate Diesel and Aral Ultimate 100, new fuel types designed to be cleaner and more economical than their predecessors while also delivering more horsepower. No cars roll in to fill up at the station. Instead, scores of motorists visit on foot to tell researchers what they think about the newly designed pumps, fuel nozzles, product leaflets and display boards.

Back in 2002 a small team of BP experts hatched a plan, codenamed Magic Flute, to create an entirely new diesel fuel. BP's German subsidiary had always been a confident innovator in the field. One of Aral's scientists, Walter Oswald, created the world's first "super fuel" back in 1924 by mixing traditional petrol with benzene. In 1987, Aral rolled out the first super diesel version in the industry. Diesel varieties with lower sulphur content and a "whisper fuel" that reduced engine noise followed.

This time it was about creating a new variety so that Aral customers could have a choice between different diesel fuels at the pump. A simple assumption was made at the outset: demand patterns are going to change. In the coming years, customers will buy cars with higher fuel efficiency and lower emissions. Legal air pollution limits will become stricter and gas guzzlers emitting large amounts of CO_2 will survive only in tiny niches. Over the long term, oil prices will rise and climate change will rank ever higher on the political agenda and in consumers' minds.

Much technological innovation was already happening around hybrid engine technology that combined fuel with electric propulsion as well as around purely electric motors. But on the fuel side things were also shifting. Hydrogen and biofuels were beginning to come into consideration as serious business cases while traditional fossil fuels were being pushed to new quality levels. This was where Aral planned to get involved.

The odds were against the project. Germany, with its high levels of expertise in car and engine manufacturing, is one of the most sophisticated fuel markets in the world. The task for Aral's team was to get a significant edge

---

About Aral

Aral is one of the most trusted brands in Germany. It has been associated with quality automotive fuels since the 1920s. Today, people also associate Aral with good food and excellent service on the go.

Every day more than 2.5 million customers visit an Aral station to refill the tank, use the carwash or purchase refreshments. In fact, some 40 percent of Aral customers stop by just to shop in the sleekly designed retail spaces, which stock a range of convenience items and Aral branded motor oils, along with coffee and food. So, in addition to being Germany's leading fuel brand marketer, Aral is also the country's third largest fast-food retailer after McDonald's and Burger King.

It's no surprise then that Aral is a "Superbrand," one of 73 brands in Germany to be awarded this designation by an independent organisation – or that for several years running Reader's Digest readers have named Aral Germany's most trusted fuel brand.

---

over numerous competitors that already offer motorists high quality regular, super and diesel versions. It was also going to be a tall order as, at first glance, there seemed to be little room for higher prices reflecting better performance and high development costs. German fuel prices were already among the highest in the EU. Furthermore, German taxes on petrol are so high that fuel producers usually earn just 8 cents per litre at most, a margin that ranks at the very bottom in Europe.

These circumstances called for a new product that palpably demonstrated its technological superiority. Pampered consumers between Hamburg and Munich would have to be won over by something really innovative.

The final result spoke for itself. In the end, Aral's engineers and scientists pushed their new fuel to performance levels that set an industry benchmark at the time. Aral Ultimate Diesel is so far the only fuel fulfilling the strict standards of the Original Equipment Manufacturers (OEM), the most influential global association of car producers.

But before its laboratories sprang into action, Aral began with extensive data mining and consumer research, putting customers under the microscope right at the pump. "We tried to find out if and how much motorists care about what they put into their tank," explains Paul Beckwith, fuels product manager at BP, "Would they pay more if fuel performance was increased really convincingly? We had to formulate exactly what customers in the defined target segment would respond to." The incoming data looked promising. No less than 37 percent of respondents said they would pay more for fuel that gets more kilometres per litre.

This data was a decisive result and a surprise to most experts in a context where it was thought there was no great room for differentiation around the performance of individual brands. But the answers were also astonishingly unambiguous regarding another customer desire: "German drivers told us they wanted a greener fuel, but also that they wouldn't be prepared to pay a premium for it unless it delivered higher performance. Thus the environmental attributes would be just the icing on the cake," says BP's Philip New who conducted the initial research run.

On the basis of these findings a decision was taken, rounding off the first step of Aral's innovation process. A fuel would have to be made that went significantly beyond the norm technologically, a greener high performance fuel that could be sold for significantly more than standard diesel.

In the prototyping steps, Aral Ultimate Diesel took shape in BP's various labs. BP's main centre of development activity is its research centre in the city of Bochum, Germany. But other expert centres such as Pangbourne in Great Britain and Naperville, Illinois in the USA, as well as independent suppliers, worked with the German team.

At this stage the project started to involve more and more people, as it had to be brought swiftly to market. While Beckwith masterminded the overall business strategy and his outline was being executed by BP's global fuels technology team in their labs, Philip New, a marketing manager who has studied the fast moving world of consumer brands in depth, and Michael Brell, who managed market entry in Germany, worked to bring the new product to Aral's pumps. Altogether eleven workstreams with attendant teams had to be formed and steered towards success.

Aral Ultimate Diesel has less frothing formation than common diesel

Aral's scientists still had a good deal of work on their hands before a patent could be registered on the new fuel under DE 10 2005 012 807. Their development work was strictly guided by the idea formulated in prior steps of the innovation process. So they knew exactly what they were after and in which direction they had to push their experiments. Standard diesel fuel carries a cetane number of 51, with BP's "Super Diesel," the diesel brand already sold through 2,400 German petrol stations, standing at 55. As fuel burns in a diesel engine by sheer mechanical compression, a higher cetane number indicates a shorter time between injection into the motor and its combustion. Faster combustion, in turn, leaves less residuals. The resulting higher cetane ratings have an immediate positive effect on the wear of an engine, emission levels and performance. Noise levels are also reduced.

Aral's experts raised the combustion speed of Aral Ultimate Diesel to the highest level in the market: a reading of 60. In parallel they also eliminated a crucial technological detail in traditional diesel production. Typically the fuel is refined at 380 °C, which routinely builds "tough" molecules. These unwanted byproducts leave valves and injection nozzles with damaging crusty residuals. Friction increases against critical motor parts and they wear out faster. But if raw diesel was processed in refineries at temperatures below 350 °C, Aral's engineers concluded correctly, all this damage could be avoided. Furthermore, lower temperature treatment would not only give the fuel an appearance of water-like transparency but also an almost complete absence of odour – easily discernible features that would help to position Aral Ultimate Diesel as a true innovation and an environmentally friendly product.

The new refining process also delivered a valuable side effect: a specific gravity that is more evenly distributed throughout the fuel, directly raising its energy content and, hence, raising its performance in combustion.

A whole range of additives also polished the new formula. Fuel additives usually help to keep viscosity at low temperatures and lessen corrosion in engines. Aral's scientists used additives in Aral Ultimate Diesel to avoid froth and make combustion cleaner, as well as putting in a detergent. These finishing touches increased the fuel flow by 430 percent during the critical early stages of fuel injection – delivering another palpable boost in performance.

Big product achievements nevertheless need meticulous marketing planning, even in Germany where Aral leads the market with a 23 percent share. A designated team dealt with the necessary brand adaptations before launch. BP's main German brand, Aral, has its individual set of propositions as has the BP brand itself, which is also visible in Germany. Both of these profiles had to be reconciled with the help of external brand agencies. The guideline: Aral Ultimate Diesel's main proposition to the consumer is better performance followed by improved environmental impact and greater efficiency. Overall, it helped the marketing of the new fuel variety that the Aral brand was already widely trusted among local consumers. Aral's fast-food business, for instance, has been voted most trusted seven times in a row.

Meanwhile, another work group was busy preparing the nitty-gritty of the actual launch. A whole raft of promotional channels had to be prepared to communicate the huge advantages offered by the new fuel. Ad campaigns

Innovation Process: Planning

In October 2003 a small project team of BP experts under the direction of Michael Brell had started work on a confidential project codenamed Magic Flute. Brell decided to divide the planning phase into eleven workstreams to cover all relevant topics for a successful market introduction.

The customer insight workstream started analysing the customer value and customer expectations and integrating them during the development of the new fuel. Members of the branding workstream worked on a branding concept for Aral Ultimate Diesel and their marketing colleagues on a comprehensive marketing plan. The price gap between the new high quality fuel and the standard fuels had to be defined, while retrofitting of the filling station network and modification of IT systems had to be meticulously planned. The team managed investments for the Ultimate production in the company's own refineries, a new supply-chain concept for the new product, smooth integration of the new Ultimate fuels into the day-to-day business of the filling stations and adaptation of the control systems.

The programme management team was the crucial interface between corporations and external network partners. The business case was the foundation for all planning and key decisions. Additionally a multi-stage approval process was established to better structure the product innovation. The advantages of this approach are obvious: the workstreams can focus on their individual topics, parallel workstreams allow for a tighter timeframe and the knowledge pool of internal and external specialists can be leveraged.

Innovation Process: Testing and Validation

Before the first motorist reached for the pump nozzle, Aral Ultimate Diesel was analysed in a final round of live tests carried out in laboratories, on motor test blocks, in single cars and with whole fleets on the road. Testers tried the fuel in virtually all available car models. External reviewers also did their own tests. Germany's Association for Technical Inspection (TÜV) kicked the tires on Aral Ultimate Diesel, as did British experts from testing firm G-Force. Standardised methods were used in both cases to create comparability.

The tests proved what the scientists and engineers had predicted. The new fuel – tested on distances up to 10,000 kilometres – boosts a car's kilowatt performance by up to 8.3 percent. This comes with significantly better acceleration. Up to 11 percent more performance is gained, while consumption is 4.5 percent lower at constant performance levels. Aral's experts calculated that a motorist who clocks 18,000 kilometres on conventional diesel fuel could get up to 810 kilometres more by refuelling with Aral Ultimate Diesel. Road tests also showed that engines emit around 38 percent less unburned hydrocarbon and roughly 27 percent less carbon monoxide, just as Aral's scientists anticipated.

needed to be conceptualised for print media, radio, television and BP's internal channels. A customer hotline had to be set up for the rollout and press events organised where cars fuelled with Aral Ultimate Diesel could be test-driven by influential automotive journalists on a racecourse.

One single team dedicated its expertise to probably the most important question of the whole innovation process. What price would be chosen for the new fuel? The team worked on the basis of initial findings that, for both a loyal "believing" Aral customer and a more skeptical one, price ranks second as long as better performance is noticeably delivered. But how to boil that down to get a concrete figure? Sets of so-called "elasticity" data on how demand would develop with rising prices were collected through another round of polls at the pumps. From that data curve it was possible to pick a definite price point. Taking into account all the available market research, Aral's experts eventually aimed at 10 cents above the Super Diesel version already being sold. Apart from delivering a return for BP, this would also ensure that multi-million euro budgets spent on research and development, reconfiguring the refining process and upgrading of petrol stations would be financially covered.

A new product can quickly lose momentum, however, if real distribution infrastructure is insufficient or not working properly. Therefore two additional groups budgeted for the hardware side of the project. Aral Ultimate Diesel was going to need new storage tanks, specially designed pumps and its own brand displays. BP's team pulled together architects and construction contractors in order to prepare the Aral station network for the big rollout day. The fuel itself needed a separate fleet of tankers to act as the backbone of the supply chain. Interim storage facilities were also needed. The closer it came to launch day, the more the operations team went into action, with work focused on the front end. Station managers had to be briefed on the new fuel's details and characteristics so they could sell it confidently to motorists. Till systems, receipt printers and roadside pylons for price information needed reprogramming.

Last but not least, Aral Ultimate Diesel would take up additional production capacity; shiny new petrol stations are no good to anyone if they run dry. How would existing refinery facilities be affected if an unusually spectacular market success created the need for extra capacity? The new brand would be distilled at BP's refinery plant in Gelsenkirchen, Germany. Creating the necessary production scope and also dealing with the Latin American partner PDSVA, which has a 50 percent stake in the plant, was the focus for yet another working group.

The different rounds of practice tests with the new petrol reflected what scientists had so far only predicted theoretically: a performance increase of up to 11 percent was gained while consumption fell by 4.5 percent.

Having successfully piloted the new fuel, BP selected 28 June 2004 as the launch date for the new product and Berlin as the first station network to be supplied. Naturally, the official rollout was fine-tuned down to the last comma.

Aral filling station

There was a sneak preview five days prior to launch for automotive journalists and, in addition, after launch, other motoring experts were quick to give their assessments. Germany's most influential touring club, ADAC, for example, subjected the fuel to its own tests, concluding, "The lower consumption compensates partly for the higher price. Refilling a 50 litre tank saves up to 3 litres. In general the new premium fuel is a boon as car manufacturers can use it as the basis for new, even more fuel-efficient engines." A further boost came from a review by motor magazine Autozeitung. In a test of similar premium fuels, among them Shell's V-Power Diesel and Total's Excellium, BP's Aral Ultimate Diesel beat its rivals by a substantial margin in all three categories.

One year after launch, Aral Ultimate Diesel was a commercial success. More than 10 percent of all diesel-based motorists in Germany bought the new product, markedly exceeding the early business case predictions. Independent studies concluded that the fuel could capture up to a fifth of the diesel market.

SCHOTT

02

A green recipe for an expanded market

Enthusiastic cooks partial to the odd Thai Dungeness Crab in Green Curry *à l'Ail Noir* and similar ambitious culinary undertakings need a stress-proof and durable mechanical *sous chef*. Glass ceramic cooktops adeptly serve this purpose, resiliently withstanding the rigours of daily use. Yet, up to now, arsenic and antimony have had to be added during production of the material to prevent bubbles building up in it. These two basic metalloids are hazardous, though they do become entirely harmless in a manufactured cooktop. Now, however, in an award winning and patented production process, German-based technology group Schott – a multinational producer of high-tech glass components – has become the first producer worldwide to completely dispense with the toxic inputs.

Schott CERAN cooktop with blue LEDs

In doing so, the company has created a totally innovative product with a compelling ecological edge. By putting sustainability at the core of its business it has also become a driving force in a progressive environmental trend. Furthermore, Schott is now also the only manufacturer able to offer consumers a choice in the colour of the LED within their cooktops. This gives its direct clients – appliance manufacturers – room for differentiation in their marketing efforts.

Glass ceramic products, as the name implies, combine the translucency of glass with the sturdiness of ceramics. The synthesis is achieved using a special baking process called ceramisation and it allows manufacturers to create glass stove cooktops. However, throughout the 40-year history of these products, manufacturers have been forced to use arsenic and antimony to prevent the build-up during production of gas bubbles that would spoil the aesthetics and make the surface porous and difficult to clean. So tiny are these gas pockets that they cannot achieve the necessary buoyancy to rise to the surface in sticky molten glass and burst into the atmosphere. This is where arsenic and antimony – which have gained notoriety in many a poisoning plot – have proved useful.

Added to the source materials, the toxic ingredients build large oxygen bubbles that absorb immobile micro-pockets and then pop, thereby purifying the panels of imperfections. Once solidified, the cooktops become crystal-clear and as smooth as any window cleaner could desire.

After three decades, black glass ceramics are still going strong. And with customers becoming increasingly eco-friendly, Schott's top management saw

About Schott

Schott is a multinational, technology-based group that has been developing and manufacturing specialty materials, components and systems for more than 125 years to help improve the way people live and work. Its main markets are household appliances, pharmaceutical industries, solar energy, electronics, optics and automotive.

The company's global sales were around € 2.3 billion in 2009, 73 percent outside Germany. Schott has 17,400 employees worldwide, 6,500 of whom are in Germany, as well as manufacturing sites and sales offices in 43 countries close to its customers in all major markets.

In order to systematically improve efficiency and customer satisfaction, management and employees align themselves to Schott's core values: accountability, market-driven innovation, technological expertise, integrity, reliability and entrepreneurship. The company's technological and economic expertise goes hand in hand with its social and environmental responsibility.

clear commercial potential in their new idea. The innovation drive was given added push by European Union regulation. Brussels aims at clearing appliances of all toxic substances in just a few years and restriction of their use in production. In EU draft directives, arsenic was already high on the list for a possible ban. Against this backdrop, Schott saw an opportunity to become a company focused entirely on sustainable products, with an innovation involving production completely free from toxic heavy metals. "Rather than lobbying in Brussels for a ban on these substances we chose to offer the consumer a new environmentally friendly product without a substantial change in price. The demand for such a product was there, which would drive new regulation anyway," says Hans-Joachim Konz, the Schott board member responsible for research and development.

It worked. In October 2009 the hundred millionth CERAN cooktop was ordered – all in all, a profitable business. "All those black panels we sell today are heavy metal free and we have already earned back our investment," says Konz.

As a welcome side effect, the innovative production process will also save hundreds of jobs at Schott's headquarters in Mainz, Germany, where it will be able to continue production uninterrupted once a ban on arsenic and antimony comes into effect. First and foremost, however, Schott introduced its environmentally friendly CERAN brand to a world market in which it was already a leader – an effective way of securing its market dominance and clearly setting itself apart from its peers as the vanguard in technology and innovation.

Schott sees great value in protecting its intellectual property against rivals. It therefore developed its new production process entirely in-house. Once the innovation was prototyped and had been through practical testing, it was immediately protected through patent filings (DE102008050263B4) in Germany, the EU und the USA to secure its full commercial potential. "The patents protect the product innovation itself, whereas the process innovations are kept as trade secrets," says Friedrich Siebers, a Materials Development Manager at Schott and key figure in this innovation. "The first experiments date back to the nineties," he recalls, "We thought about how to improve people's work and life environments. This was really the starting point. We then began with basic research and covered new ground over the years. And we still follow the same goal."

In essence, the production process innovation was a new melting technology involving a new system of heat and energy management driven by an electromagnetic heating source. This technology allows for higher flexibility regarding the specific mixture of chemical additives and is able to bring glass ceramic panels to a highly purified quality standard without the need for arsenic or antimony. Agents that eliminate gas bubbles are still required, but Schott invented a viable formula built around environmentally harmless tin oxide. The new non-toxic chemical recipe's main ingredient is simply quartz

Raw materials for glass ceramic cooktops

CERAN production: ceramisation

sand – a natural product. In a sophisticated physical procedure, the company's development engineers managed to arrange different crystal formations during ceramisation in the furnace.

The result is nothing less than spectacular: Schott is able to save almost 200 tonnes of toxic metalloids a year. Production and disposal of the new product do no harm to air, water or soil at all. "Thanks to the new melting technology we are exceeding European Union regulations and already meeting future ecological standards," says Stefan-Marc Schmidt, Vice President of Marketing and Sales for Schott Home Tech. But the truly remarkable thing is that the innovative process produces a glass ceramic quality that beats earlier versions for robustness, heat transmission and temperature resistance. This is a big step forward as it means that the new cooktop is hardly affected by aging and virtually indestructible if used properly. These features, which are all part of the clean production processes, form a powerful marketing lever with environmentally conscious customers – a rapidly expanding market. Market researchers at GfK, for example, have found that 48 percent of German consumers say they would pay more for environmentally friendly appliances.

A smart new aesthetic quality was also achieved at the same time. The new glass formula allowed transmission of light spectrums other than reddish ones for the first time. Since coming to market at the beginning of the seventies, glass ceramic tops' cooking plate, LED gauges and display lights had been limited to a narrow band of red, brown and orange shades. This was because the cooktop panels, most of them around 4 millimetres thick, had to be chemically configured so that the infrared heat for cooking could pass through it quickly, which ruled out other chromatic shades.

Innovation Success Factors

Satisfaction of a true customer demand

By providing a blue LED option, Schott was able to satisfy a true customer demand. The company had been hearing from their customers in Europe's household appliance industry and thinking about colour for quite some time. This insight had been revealed and boosted by internal brainstorming workshops, extensive market research (such as idea-generation workshops with clients and focus groups) and collaboration with external trendscout agencies. "We will keep working to achieve the colourations our customers are asking for in different ways. After all, differentiation is what we are seeking to offer," says Lutz Klippe, Schott's Product Innovation Manager.

Many of today's devices have blue displays – car speedometers, for example. Household appliance manufacturers have also been giving a lot of thought to how to stand out in the marketplace by offering different colour options, e.g. blue displays for ovens, refrigerators, microwaves and washing machines.

Presence of an innovator authority

This impressive case of a combined product and process innovation shows how important the innovator authority is for the innovation process. Without the full backing of the board and chief executive officer, CERAN might still be just an invention stuck somewhere in Schott's labs. "Only the board can take the decision to launch a basic research program on this scale. And only the chief executive can carry responsibility and risk when a company like Schott pours so much talent and money into a new idea. It is only right from the top that you can make all your departments get in step to market and sell the new product once it is there," says Hans-Joachim Konz, a businessman with a pioneer spirit.

Colour has already begun to be more widely used on appliances in general, including glass ceramic cooktops. Manufacturers have thought a lot about how to generate emotions with regard to their products and brands. "We've been hearing from our customers in Europe's appliance industry about colour for quite some time," says Schmidt. Shades of blue in this context are considered especially "cool." Big appliance manufacturers are currently fitting other kitchen appliances such as dishwashers or washing machines with mainly blue light displays. CERAN cooktops can now take their place in this environment, making them really stand out in the marketplace.

In addition to its innovations in production processes and the product itself, Schott set up a shrewd and innovative marketing push towards the end user. Its actual buyers are big domestic appliances manufacturers who, as a result of Schott's innovation, were able to make innovations in their own marketing to their customers. The company struck co-branding and ingredient branding alliances with several large appliance producers – Whirlpool in the USA and Europe, among others. As a result, these producers now put stickers on their cooktops highlighting either the heavy-metal-free production method or directly referring to Schott's CERAN brand. This allows these companies to take on Schott's new cooktops' green image themselves. In return, Schott is able to reach out directly to the end customer.

"The eco-friendly Schott CERAN cooktops fit perfectly with our sustainability strategy, in which we emphasise energy and resource efficiency as well as responsibility towards the environment," says Pierfranca Brossa, Value Brand and Cooperations Manager at Whirlpool Europe. Whirlpool was the first to promote the sustainable aspects of Schott CERAN cooktops in its marketing materials, resulting in a perfectly planned and executed integrated communication campaign.

The innovation may soon be transferred to some of Schott's other markets. The company is currently testing the new production process' suitability for other glass ceramic products such as fire protection glass in stoves.

Positioning of eco-friendly CERAN in the marketing material of Whirlpool's Bauknecht brand

Marathon

03

A new safety solution

As recently as 1987, British coal miners kept canaries in the pits to alert them to the presence of explosive methane or poisonous carbon monoxide. When the birds stopped singing and screeched in panic, miners knew they had to evacuate quickly. There are still dangers in the natural resources sector and efficient gas detection, in particular, is still a necessity, but the technology has improved dramatically since the days when canaries were used. In a remarkable process innovation, Marathon Petroleum Company LP, a subsidiary of Marathon Oil Company (NYSE: MRO), has helped develop a new, potentially life-saving technology at its Robinson, Illinois refinery. At this refinery site, workers can now be continuously monitored through a wireless device that not only helps keep them safe, but also provides an infrastructure to help improve productivity in the field.

Marathon refinery

A worker protection innovation drive was started by the Refinery Manager at the time, John Swearingen. As a result, the Robinson plant started looking into whether an intelligent continuous "man-down" monitor system was available in the industry. "We had a clear vision of a device to monitor and locate people but there was nothing available on the market that would suit our needs," explains Kevin Bogard, Refining Operations and Technology Manager.

The standard gas monitoring devices on the market today are typically single gas detectors that measure H_2S, SO_2 and CO. They are routinely given to workers and contractors at oil refineries, chemical or waste-water plants, on cargo ships and oil platforms, and in agricultural silos, mines, or utility plants. Their use can be effective at warning the worker that gas concentrations have exceeded a certain level and their widespread introduction has been reflected in falling accident rates. However, the monitors' chirp or beep typically can only be heard by the person wearing it. Such a localised warning creates its own problem because locating workers in the event of an emergency becomes a challenge unless rescue personnel are close enough to hear the alert or can actually see the person – and that assumes it is even known that rescue is required. For these reasons industrial plant operators wanted a portable safety device that could report back to control rooms the basic kind of emergency that was taking place and the type of gas involved.

The innovation had to meet three criteria: reliability, ease of use and affordability. To investigate the innovative ideas that came out of Robinson, Marathon worked with Accenture to create a consortium of vendors that could

About Marathon

Marathon Oil Company is an integrated international energy company engaged in exploration and production; oil sands mining; integrated gas; and refining, marketing and transportation operations. Marathon, which is based in Houston, has principal operations in the United States, Angola, Canada, Equatorial Guinea, Indonesia, Libya, Norway, Poland, the Iraqi Kurdistan region and the United Kingdom. Marathon is the fourth largest United States-based integrated oil company and the nation's fifth largest refiner.

provide components for a new monitoring system. These included Cisco Systems, Industrial Scientific and AeroScout.

Refinery workers were involved in the development of the new system from an early stage. It was important for workers to know that the new device was not for personnel tracking but rather a mechanism that could potentially save lives. Employees were invited to attend and give advice during prototyping and testing. "The key user components were reviewed by Marathon employees: the displays, the buttons, the alarm functions," says Ken Johnson from Accenture who coordinated the project on the consultants' side.

Oil refineries are sprawling complexes with systems of pipes, vessels, pumps, tanks and valves. The predominance of dense steel and concrete structures, equipment, pipes and tanks made developing a wireless system difficult, but not insurmountable for those with the proper experience.

The innovation team aimed at developing a safety system that could monitor and report H_2S, CO, O_2, LEL, NO_2 and SO_2 within one device. The idea was to communicate using a wireless network technology that is widely used by logistics companies to monitor the stream of parcels through their delivery chain in real-time. The moving parts of the system, in this case the refinery workers, were fitted with a portable safety device containing a small Wi-Fi RFID tag that could send signals across the Cisco wireless infrastructure. The Cisco Access Point locations were designed using Accenture's patent pending design approach, which takes into consideration enhanced location capability at a reduced cost. In initial tests, prototype detector devices were simply taped to Wi-Fi tags. This showed that the wireless technology could cover an area with sustained data transmission. During these tests, the team also saw the first data on gas type and concentration, measured by the monitors coming into the central control room via the network.

"When we did the first test, the location quality was actually very good," Ken Johnson of Accenture recalls. The initial testing was performed on two process units on the Robinson site, a Diesel Hydrotreating Unit and a Gasoline Desulfurisation Unit. Both were fitted with 13 Cisco outdoor access points in

Gasoline
Desulfurisation Unit

all, covering them with an integrated wireless signal. Information regarding gas levels and location were sent every five seconds to the operator console. The new gas detectors provided by Industrial Scientific were clipped to the workers' lapels. The Wi-Fi tags were supplied by AeroScout leveraging technology made by Cisco Systems. The safety system has been registered for US patents (12/634,110, 12/847,718, PCT/US10/43972).

Once the new system is up and running, controllers will know at any given moment where employees are working, where they are heading and what

Innovation Performance Factor

Building and maintenance of networks and alliances

Innovations that achieve market success without partners, alliances, networks or other cooperation types are rare. Networks and alliances offer access to useful, complementary goods and skills. In this case, the solution would not have been achievable by a single company. Accenture worked with Marathon to develop the solution by pulling together a consortium of best-in-class vendors including Cisco, Industrial Scientific and AeroScout. AeroScout's Wi-Fi tag was used and embedded in the Industrial Scientific 4 gas detection device. This device works in conjuction with the Cisco wireless network to transmit data from the detector to the operator in the control room. This technology alliance was useful to Marathon in all stages of the innovation process – from planning to execution. Successful collaborations of this sort depend on win-win thinking and aligned objectives on the part of all parties involved.

they may be exposed to. "The advantage of this new communication is tremendous," says Ken Johnson. An event can be spotted, located and the gas involved identified without the victim doing anything. If any alerts are received at the refinery control room, the individual is spoken to immediately via radio if they have one and other workers are deployed to verify they are OK.

The lapel monitoring device also has a panic button that can be pressed by the wearer if health problems arise unrelated to gas leaks – broken legs or cardiovascular issues, for instance. A motion sensor also detects when a worker stops moving for a period of time, triggering a local alarm to alert the individual concerned. If motion is not sensed within a predefined time after this, a second alert will be sent to the central control room.

In general, the devices could allow for a higher degree of efficiency in mass evacuation as board operators now know who is in their units and can help confirm that employees have cleared the area. "It is also quicker to identify leaks and to report them if you have 100 people with smart devices in the plant," says Don McCord, Operations Manager.

The new system has proven to be very cost effective to install. Once in place, the infrastructure may also be used to improve efficiency in numerous other ways such as tracking high value mobile equipment, creating video links with people in the field, increasing work productivity through the use of handheld devices and many more.

EVONIK

04

Merging the molecules of knowledge

"Nanotronics" is a word that might make you want to reach for a magnifying glass – if not your electron microscope. But hang on! Nanotronics is the name of something very visible to the naked eye: a low-rise and very stylish building. Fitted with huge glass panels, it was erected five years ago by Evonik Industries, a specialty chemicals producer with an edge in high technology. The modernism and transparency of the building located in an industrial park just outside Marl, Germany, symbolise an extremely efficient and flexible way of arranging research within a science-driven company. Its organisational innovation, dubbed a focused science-to-business approach, has earned Evonik significantly faster development times and growth.

An Evonik Science-to-Business Centre

The lab compound, one of three so-called Science-to-Business Centres at Marl, houses around fifty scientists. Nanotronics researches ultramodern materials involving nano-particles. The aim is to create coatings that can be printed to form microelectronic tags, a novelty that could soon take over from good old bar codes on the day-to-day things we buy. The other Science-to-Business Centres – Bio and Eco2 – work on biotechnology, energy efficiency, and climate protection.

However, pioneering high-tech products are not the real stars here. It's more the innovative set-up of the research processes behind them, which involves researchers and developers from industry, academia, and research institutions whose flexible work set-up is managed by Evonik's strategic research unit Creavis Technologies & Innovation.

In 2008 Evonik set itself the target of becoming the most profitable and creative specialty chemicals supplier around in only five years. Research and development play a crucial role in achieving this aim. In a nutshell, Creavis Technologies & Innovation has opened up a new research process, bringing together experts from Evonik's 2,300 scientists and teaming them up in focused research groups for specific projects. The success of this new approach is palpable, resulting in shorter lab stages and a significant increase in innovative products and solutions.

Economically this is vital for the company. Chemicals are by far Evonik's most important business area. They generate 75 percent of sales and, with more than 20,000 registered patent applications and a research budget of

---

About Evonik

With its three profitable business areas (chemicals, energy and real estate) Evonik Industries is active in attractive markets. In 2009 it had over 39,000 employees and generated sales of around €13.1 billion and an operating profit (EBITDA) of more than €2 billion.

Evonik's chemicals group has a long, eventful history and deep roots. It all started in 1873 with the Aktiengesellschaft Deutsche Gold und Silber Scheideanstalt, which was founded in Frankfurt. The company officially became Degussa AG in 1980. In February 2003, Essen-based RAG AG acquired 46.48 percent of Degussa shares. By mid-2004, this share had increased to 50.1 percent. The corporation fully acquired all Degussa shares in September 2006. One year later, on September 12, 2007, Degussa became the chemicals group in the new creative industry group known as Evonik Industries AG.

---

about €300 million per year, chemicals are the group's innovation drivers, generating around €2 billion profit per annum.

In hardly any other sector has the pressure to innovate become higher than in the chemicals industry. Scientists in the laboratories of leading companies are constantly developing entirely new product ranges and applications based on future-oriented technologies such as nano- and biotechnology. With innovations ranging from ultra-thin displays that can be rolled up and folded like paper to optimised microorganisms that generate fuel from straw and wood scrap, very little appears to be impossible in the world of specialty chemicals and biochemistry.

Typically, chemical companies such as Evonik now generate 80 percent of their sales from market leading products and 20 percent from successful inventions less than five years old. Yet development processes are often still extraordinarily time-consuming in this sector, particularly in specialty chemicals. More than ten years often pass from the initial idea to market launch. Given these time spans, the organisation and speed of a research process can become decisive in the global competition race.

In traditional development processes, research departments are divided along the lines of the company's business areas. On the basis of renewable raw materials, for example, researchers might develop a novel insulating material for the construction industry. Only at a relatively late stage would project managers be called in, at which point they would present the new development to customers, after which it would be adapted to customer requirements. These adaptation processes cost a lot of time and money – and also increase the risk of a competitor bringing a similar solution to market faster.

Evonik has long since abandoned this old-fashioned model. Investments in research and development are now handled much more flexibly: the higher the customer benefits expected from a new development, the higher is the research budget. As much as 85 percent of the total research budget is invested for operationally driven research such as line extensions, product adaptations or process improvements.

The remaining 15 percent is earmarked for strategic research activities in "technologies, applications, and system solutions for markets of the future with above-average growth rates," as Evonik puts it. The Creavis unit was established for these research activities in the medium to high risk range – meaning, they have a medium to high risk of failure in the market.

In developing new businesses, Creavis basically follows the classic innovation process structure, from initial idea to market launch. But projects are further segmented into one of two different contexts, depending on innovation value and financial risk.

Projects of medium risk for market failure or of particularly fundamental importance extending across business-unit boundaries are handled in so-called Project Houses. Here, over a period of three years, researchers from different business units within Evonik come together and work jointly on the research topics. Half of the finance for the Project Houses comes from corporate and the other half from the participating business units.

After the three-year period, and, ideally, completion of the project, the researchers return to their business units, taking with them the knowledge and expertise they have acquired. Products and technologies developed in the Project Houses are usually then commercialised in the business units. In a very recent development, Project Houses are also gaining geographical spread. In 2011 the first Project House outside Germany will be launched.

High risk research topics in areas that are completely new to Evonik are handled in the Science-to-Business Centres such as Nanotronics in Marl. These centres are based on the concept of integrating all research and development activities along the process – from fundamental research through

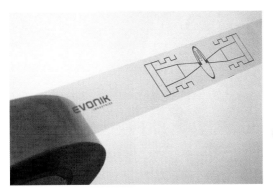

RFID-antenna and Li-Tec-cell

Innovation Core Module: Organisation and Governance

Evonik's Science-to-Business Centres illustrate how aligning organisation and governance with a company's innovation strategy can improve realisation of the innovation agenda. The structure of the centres allows employees in R&D to switch easily between projects – thus accelerating delivery of new products to market, which is critically important in a fast moving industry such as chemicals.

Innovation Enabling Module: Knowledge Management

Innovation is, of course, heavily dependent on knowledge exchange. The Science-to-Business Centres' collaborative set-up supports this. After completing a project, the researchers, enriched by interdisciplinary knowledge, move on to their next assignment. Additionally, Evonik has built and maintained a network with universities and outside research institutions, allowing for further deepening of knowledge.

The centres allow employees to think beyond the firm's traditional boundaries. The company's internal market mechanism for combining best ideas with best resources is also a key success factor in Evonik's R&D organisation and governance.

product development to pilot production – under one single roof. The aim is rapid development of new businesses all the way to production of complete systems for the end user. Collaboration with academic and research institutions as equal and integrated partners allows the deepening of knowledge in basic research. In developing products, the researchers work with potential customers right from the start in order to understand their requirements better and find adequate solutions.

The Science-to-Business Centres are equipped with all the technology needed for development of innovations, from research laboratories to test centres for setting up pilot production plants. Scientists from the company and from academia interact with suppliers and customers in buildings with distinctively open architecture.

"About 80 percent of all innovations come about as a result of personal communication and not by telephone or e-mail," says Günter Henn, architect and creator of the futuristic building in Marl. The innovation- and communication-friendly architecture facilitates the forging of alliances and networks across subject and departmental boundaries.

Although it opened only in 2005, Nanotronics, the oldest of Evonik's Science-to-Business Centres, already boasts impressive results. Its researchers have, for example, developed a ceramic separator that dramatically improves the safety and performance of large lithium-ion batteries – an important milestone in the development of electric cars for everyday use. So promising is the product that Evonik and Daimler have now agreed on an ambitious collaborative project: along with Li-Tec Battery, they are developing a cutting-edge energy storage device. On the basis of Evonik's lithium-ion technology and Daimler's automotive expertise, both conglomerates will research, develop and produce battery cells and systems in Germany. As early as 2012 Daimler plans to launch cars fuelled by Evonik batteries. On its way to technological leadership in this area Evonik has invested about €80 million over the last few years, resulting in high-tech battery cells that can be produced on a commercial scale and are markedly superior to competitive products in many important respects.

Successes like these, of course, heap expectations on the other two Science-to-Business Centres, which started later. One of them, Bio, set up in 2007, carries out research in the area of so-called white biotechnology, focusing on sustainable production processes such as fermentation and bio-catalysis based on renewable raw materials. The goal is to synthesise bio-based materials with outstanding functionalities or significant cost advantages. Within the centre, different competence clusters include development of high-performance polymers and production of ingredients for cosmetics and anti-ageing products.

Production of Separion® separator

Innovation Success Factors

Strictly continous innovation process

To be successful, innovations must be closely managed throughout the process – from early idea to market success – and clear ownership of responsibilities identified. The Evonik example clearly shows the strict management of the innovation process by various responsible persons and teams – so-called "process owners." Depending on the degree of novelty and the research topic's financial risk, projects are assigned to either Evonik's Project Houses or its Science-to-Business Centres. Cross-divisional research topics with medium risk are assigned to the Project Houses at Evonik's Hanau-Wolfgang facilities with a set time period of three years. The high risk research topics that go into new areas are assigned to the Science-to-Business Centres located in Marl. To limit the overall risk, portfolio management counterbalances the projects. Portfolio management obtains its data from a five-stage process: from idea, evaluation and project development, to assessment of the results and transfer to market.

Building and maintenance of networks and alliances

The Science-to-Business Centres offer an ideal framework for cooperation with internal and external partners. The benefit to Evonik is they acquire deeper knowledge in fundamental research. The centres are also financially supported by the state of North-Rhine Westphalia and co-financed by the European Union.

Establishment of an environment that demands and promotes innovation

The Science-to-Business concept is based on uniting all the research and development activities along the value chain under one roof – from basic research and product development to pilot plant production. The innovation process is not just on paper or on screen, but is brought to life in the architecture of the building and the set-up of the office space so that the employees can live and breathe innovation every day.

The newest Science-to-Business Centre, Eco², was launched in 2008. It pools the available Evonik Group skills in the area of energy efficiency and climate protection. The focus is particularly on medium-term, economical, and attractive products and services with high CO_2 reduction potential both for customers and in Evonik's own processes.

Iberdrola

05

Making the business case for the planet's future

The many colourful accounts of Ignacio Sánchez Galán, Chairman and Chief Executive Officer of Iberdrola, describe a man on a mission, a visionary business leader and a highly energetic innovator. Numerous accolades have been heaped on the charismatic Spaniard who, by changing a whole set of existing processes and many elements of the classic utilities business model, has almost single-handedly turned Iberdrola into a green standard bearer in the energy sector. A fast thinker with a strong voice and exuberant gestures, Galán clicks with people, hugs politicians, calls Mahatma Ghandi his biggest inspiration and builds his management style on the mantra, "Be commercially enlightened."

The 60-year old engineer from Salamanca has injected his personal style into his company. In nine years at Iberdrola's helm, he has shifted the Iberian utility towards sustainability and a new growth path.

Adopting new technologies ahead of the curve was key to the strategy. While rivals tended to see sustainability as a nice-to-have, Galán declared it a *conditio sine qua non* as long ago as 2001 and has since systematically rebuilt Iberdrola's business DNA around it. The Spanish company, which began life in hydroelectric generation a century ago, was the first in its sector to whole-heartedly acknowledge climate change. It stands out today not only as one of the four or five largest global energy companies but also as the world largest wind energy producer with a turbine capacity of around 12,500 megawatts at the end of 2010.

Iberdrola Renovables, Iberdrola's sustainable subsidiary, is primarily engaged in the development, construction, operation and exploitation of power plants that use renewable energy sources, as well as in the sale of electric energy. Additionally, the company is involved in researching and developing such technologies as marine biomass and tidal energy. Its facilities include wind, mini-hydroelectric and thermo-solar energy power stations with operations established in North, Central and South America, Europe, Africa, the Middle East and Asia. It also has natural gas storage businesses in North America.

While wind is the company's primary innovation focus, Galán believes that future energy needs will not be met by a single source but rather a mosaic of

About Iberdrola

Iberdrola, S.A., together with its subsidiaries, engages in producing, switching, retailing, and distributing electricity and gas. The company primarily generates nuclear, hydroelectric, combined cycle gas and wind power. It also offers raw materials or primary energies required for electric power generation, energy, engineering, computer, and telecommunications services, services relating to the internet, urban and gas retailing services, regasification, transmission or distribution services, as well as other gas storage services, assistance and support services, and real estate and other related services. The company operates in nearly 40 countries, serves around 28 million customers and employs around 33,000 people. In 2009 its EBIT increased by 5.8 percent to €4.5 billion with revenues of €24.6 billion.

clean and renewable options. He has therefore built a diverse portfolio of energy assets – wind, solar, hydro and natural gas (the cleanest of the fossil fuels). Around 30 percent of Iberdrola's capacity currently stems from gas-fired power plants, 27 percent from renewables and 22 percent from hydroelectricity.

Having set the company on a green path a decade ago, Galán took a decisive step in 2007 with a strategy aimed at diversification and consolidating Iberdrola among the top global utilities. His vision was "back to basics" – concentration on the company's core competences – through three major initiatives.

First, he grew Iberdrola through two significant takeovers. By doing so he not only secured the basis for more growth in sustainable energy production, but also ensured that the company would survive independently in the fierce dog-eat-dog consolidation wave that has swept the international utility sector over recent years.

He identified two companies that would make perfect partners for his strategy. ScottishPower, which already had significant wind energy activities in place, was acquired in 2007 for €17 billion. A year later, he agreed a €6 billion deal for the friendly integration of Energy East in the United States, a company distributing gas and electricity to around 3 million customers in five northeastern states. Both deals were quantum leaps and, from being the 19th largest world utility by market capitalisation when Galán took over, the company is now in the top five.

Second, he was aware that the group's "green" business culture needed a new and secluded home to flourish. It was for this reason that in 2007 he created the subsidiary, Iberdrola Renovables, into which the company's wind and other renewable businesses would be spun-off. This allowed him to demonstrate the market success of his idea and create a solid basis for further development while spreading the risk. Moreover the separated business unit allowed for the creation of a distinct culture.

From the beginning it was clear that Iberdrola's renewables business had to grow in order to achieve critical mass in sustainable energy generation and gain a firm foothold in the market. The acquisition of ScottishPower in 2007 brought with it a major wind power portfolio in the United States that has since been aggressively expanded in a favourable regulatory environment to total 4,300 MW with a project pipeline of over 20,000 MW. In Europe, the official commitment to cut carbon-dioxide emissions by a fifth over the next decade, reduce energy consumption by the same amount and meet 20 percent of its energy needs from renewable resources has provided a strong incentive for Iberdrola's investment strategy in wind power.

Risks that could potentially affect its growth plans still remain. Many countries still have work to do in regulating energy demand from wind, solar, water and biomass – which typically sell at higher prices than power from traditional sources. Iberdrola Renovables could also be affected if, in response to climate change, there is a major shift in public opinion towards other sources such as nuclear power.

But Galán argues that Iberdrola's single-minded investment in green energy not only sets it apart from competitors but also sends a signal to regulators and society as a whole about its long-term dedication to sustainability. This dedication in turn helps to keep the green trend on track in society. The company's close communication and interaction with regulators is essential for its

Ignacio Sánchez Galán,
Chairman and Chief Executive
Officer of Iberdrola

Innovation Success Factors

Active management of social, political and legal parameters

As one of the cleanest European energy producers, Iberdrola is positioning itself as a credible, committed leader in the global energy market. It understands that social, political and legal barriers have to be identified at an early stage of the innovation process and are subject to continuous observation, anticipation and management. Additionally, the company's leadership knows that cooperative relationships with stakeholders are vital to ensuring that its investments in new technologies, acquisitions and R&D produce a sustainable return over the long run. Therefore, the company actively manages its stakeholders and participates in public policy, collaborates with NGOs and contributes to the wellbeing of communities in which it operates.

For example, the close support of the UK government has been highly beneficial. In 2010 the group's Scottish subsidiary, ScottishPower was chosen as finalist in the tender for the development of a commercial scale carbon capture and storage plant and in the same year the company announced that it will develop one of the largest offshore wind farms in the world in the UK with a capacity of up to 7,200 megawatts.

Iberdrola could be vulnerable to changing political winds. A shift in public opinion on climate change and carbon emissions, for example, would have an impact on its growth plans. But the company's sizeable investments and strategy of open dialogue send an unequivocal message to regulators and other stakeholders about its long-term dedication to sustainable energy.

Rigorous management of the business case

Detailed business cases are a vital part of every investment decision. The company's management looks very carefully at all investments and they are rigorously evaluated against a set of evaluation criteria. Additionally, Iberdrola has acquired like-minded firms with assets that complement its portfolio and invests in new technologies that broaden its capacity to meet diverse customer needs. As a reflection of its focus on projects with long-term return horizons, Iberdrola's renewables business has for example increased its EBITDA sixfold to €1,508 million between 2004 and 2010.

Presence of an innovator authority

Iberdrola is a good example of innovation that is clearly driven by the chief executive officer. Ignacio Galán's leadership has galvanised a cultural transformation at Iberdrola and won the respect of unions, politicians and environmental protection organisations.

Before joining Iberdrola in 2001, Galán had proven his entrepreneurial spirit already as the CEO of Airtel Movil, one of Spain's first private telecommunications companies, which, when sold to Vodafone in 2000, had almost seven million customers.

He created the innovation-friendly environment within Iberdrola and the sense, internally, that this would be the basis for its future success. The company's transformation is seen as a direct result of his visionary character. "He made the difference," an associate remembers, "Iberdrola was perceived as a fairly unambitious company prior to Galán joining."

innovative business model since energy policies either foster or undermine the profitability of clean and renewable technologies. Galán's unambiguous green commitment has bought the company a seat at the table where energy policies are decided.

Iberdrola also argues that once consumers understand the true cost of energy, they can make decisions on reducing consumption. "Championing this logic has been among Iberdrola's biggest themes in recent years. The world needs more energy efficiency and this may mean reducing the amount of electricity consumed," says Galán.

Iberdola's green image is borne out by hard scientific facts. Among the large utilities, the company has established itself as the cleanest electric energy producer in Europe according to neutrally ascertained data. It creates 289 grams of CO_2 per kilowatt-hour of energy, where the European average is 380 grams. "According to our own estimates, we often provide energy with half as much carbon content as the average utilities company in Europe," says Galán.

The third initiative was to ensure Galán that customer needs were at the forefront of the company's thinking. This went hand in hand with a programme of initiatives aimed at supporting communities where the company operates. Just recently the Board of Directors created a Corporate Social Responsibility Committee aimed at supervising these activities, making Iberdrola one of the few major Spanish companies to have done so.

The company can use its credibility to forge partnerships outside its sector. Traditionally improbable allies of big energy companies have been chosen as important ingredients in Iberdrola's sustainability strategy. Its subsidiary ScottishPower, for example, engages with the World Wildlife Fund (WWF), Friends of the Earth and other environmental groups. At the same time, employees at ScottishPower and Energy East, now renamed Iberdrola USA, actively engage with communities in which they operate to help develop economic activity there.

These efforts have paid off. Iberdrola is the only utility in the world that is found in all 10 editions of the Dow Jones Sustainability Index and, for four years in a row, Global 100 has listed it among the 100 most sustainable companies in the world.

Yet, sustainability, in Galán's view, is more than a business opportunity focused on environmentally minded customers. It must also be sewn tightly into the fabric of the company's collective mind, from the way investment decisions are screened for their environmental merits, to progressive parental leave policies. The company measures its green credentials in its own business processes and product range meticulously against several benchmarks. Not only has it done away with paper-based sustainability reports – they are published on CD now – it also puts its employees through extensive training to reinforce a common sustainability mindset throughout the company.

Education on computer-based learning systems has increased fourfold in the past eight years. Staff spend 1,100,853 hours using these programmes annually. These training methods have proved an important platform for establishing a consistent understanding of sustainability issues internally. "We have improved everyone's knowledge around eco-efficiency, biodiversity and sustainability. All employees must know how we expect them to complete their work from an environmental point of view and they are examined externally by auditors," Galán says.

Hand in hand with these sustainability initiatives, Iberdrola is actively involved in pioneering new technology aimed at creating a clean energy framework for the future. This includes smart grids, which it is installing in Spain, the UK and North America, and electric vehicles for which it is providing charging networks as part of projects in Glasgow and various locations around Spain.

The company has effectively shrugged off the traditional stereotype of a utilities firm – that of a bureaucratic, polluting monolith with a monopolistic detachment from public opinion – and fashioned itself into a force for green progress in the global energy market.

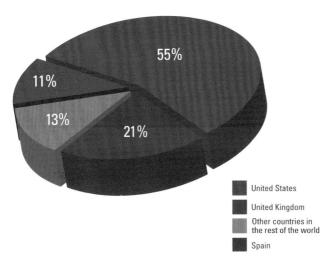

United States

United Kingdom

Other countries in the rest of the world

Spain

Distribution of gross investments planned for the 2010–2012 period: €9,000 million

Dow Corning: XIAMETER® Brand

06

Making pricing fit for purpose

At first glance it could be a website for a no-frills airline. xiameter. com has a simple design, an arresting, industrial orange colour scheme and explains itself in snappy language illustrated with loose, cartoony line drawings. You probably can, as it claims, order your industrial quantities of shampoo additive, glass sealant or cooling liquid virtually between sips in your coffee break. But while it might all seem like frivolous fun to the casual browser, it is doubtless a lot more than that for Dow Corning. In launching a highly profitable online sales channel, the US-based specialty chemicals giant has managed to overhaul its pricing model and customer segmentation in one of the most effective business model innovations in its industry, turning it into a powerful off- and online supplier.

When Dow Corning launched its online portal and eponymous new low-cost brand in 2002, both actions were triggered by crisis. In the 1990s the company, after years of solid growth averaging about 15 percent per annum, had seen its business model lose power. Worse, by the end of the decade, a global recession was raging with a currency crisis coming in its wake. It dawned on Gary Anderson, chief executive officer at the company, that Dow Corning needed a complete new edge on the market in order to regain its old strength. Anderson, who threw his full authority behind the creation of xiameter.com did so because he realised that the familiar trade landscape for silicone products had changed drastically.

New competitors had sprung up right, left and center – pushing prices ruthlessly downwards. Going the way specialty chemicals typically go commercially, standard silicones had matured over the past 65 years. Silicone is one of the most versatile industrial materials, widely used in sectors such as construction, body care, automotive and chemicals. Dow Corning acknowledged the fact that mature silicone – in its simpler varieties – had become a mass product. It was still sometimes used for innovation, but customers were no longer willing to pay Dow Corning's higher prices. This was a lesson Dow Corning found difficult to acknowledge quickly. "In general, chemicals companies are often focused on pure product innovation. The success of the XIAMETER brand shows business model innovations work there as well," says Shelley Bausch, who now heads the XIAMETER business model and was responsible for the recent relaunch of the online portal in 2009.

About XIAMETER

In 2002, Dow Corning realised customers were asking for an easier and more affordable way to buy standard silicones, so they created it in the form of the XIAMETER brand. Today, with an expanded product lineup and a powerful sales website, the promise of this revolutionary buying model has become a reality – winning attention not only from customers but also from industry observers including the Harvard Business Review. From the comfort of their desks and armchairs, customers can now browse and choose from over 2,100 standard silicones – available online or through a local distributor.

In times of economic turbulence few executives in any company would have the guts to revamp a whole business model. Don Sheets, chief financial officer of Dow Corning and the hands-on innovator who pushed through xiameter.com from early planning to launch in 2002, says, "In this environment most board members would typically rely on their core business. I guess that only ten percent really focus on innovation as the way out."

But Dow Corning had very little choice. The company, based in Midland, Michigan, has been the global household name in its field for decades. A leader in silicone science, it had for a long time comfortably commanded a market share of around 35 percent. Silicone was lucrative because it went – and still goes – into almost everything in everyday life. It makes hair easy to comb, gives raincoats "breathability" and seals cracks in buildings, to name just a few among hundreds of applications. As commercial products, silicones had been around for less than 70 years. Dow Corning was established in 1943 with the mission of exploring the material's scientific and economic potential, since which time it had developed numerous interesting and diverse products. Its assortment still amounts to over 7,500 different strands of silicone items.

During its best years, Dow Corning was driven by a combination of ambitious science and sophisticated customer dedication, wooing customers through service as much as product. Its engineers and chemists aimed their work at the technical buyer, someone who needed something very special, technologically ambitious and tailored to address a highly individual problem. A point arrived where the company was coming up with individual formulae for many of these buyers. It became a matter of pride to go the extra mile in order to find and mix exactly the right polydimethylsiloxane fluids or special acetoxy sealants. Strategic alliances were even formed with clients to develop new products. Dow Corning's specialists worked as advisors at customer sites and the company went so far as to maintain local delivery centres in joint management with buyers who enjoyed around-the-clock, just-in-time delivery. Extensive practical tests were also offered and advice given in customers'

Shelly Bausch, Global Executive
Director, XIAMETER

Don Sheets, Chief Financial Officer,
Dow Corning

mother tongues on every aspect of the product, right down to disposal issues and health and safety – a huge effort for a global company active in many different countries.

All this highly organised coordination was born out of a key underlying assumption: involvement makes customers loyal. The economic crisis made the situation all too clear: the cost of this business model was no longer sustainable for standard silicone products. Anyway, customer demand had changed and they were no longer willing to pay a premium.

In the faltering economy, a new customer segment seemed to have emerged, one that no longer had much desire for individual service. Instead they apparently just wanted a standard product at a low price. These customers knew how to use standard silicones and no longer wanted to pay a bundled price that covered both the product and all the services. Sheets recalls, "With new competitors coming online, the severe overall cost pressures at the time clearly made people demand more product for less."

"Speciality chemical companies often do not understand what their customers really want and need," says Sheets. He launched a profound examination of market and product segments, bringing to light what had long gone unnoticed: some customers know exactly what they want and how to use the products. For them silicone is just a bulk commodity. They want to buy and go.

From a detailed client survey, greater nuance emerged. Most customers were still interested in tapping Dow Corning's vast technical expertise and in developing new products in close cooperation with their supplier. A second set of buyers wanted to work with the company to improve the usage of products for their individual problems. They were willing to pay for research and development projects towards new products or wanted new application innovation for off-the-shelf products. A third group wanted the company solely to help control costs in their own production processes, for example by improving downtimes on manufacturing equipment to lessen the need for maintenance. And finally there was that completely new breed, the economic buyer described above, who simply said: all we want is four simple things: high quality, reliability, little to no service and the lowest possible price – and that's all!

From a more detailed cost-analysis point of view, the old model was no longer viable. The one-size-fits-all approach has a problem: customers who are happy to use all the services start to erode profitability as customers with no appetite for service defect to lower priced propositions offered by rivals. Finding the accurate price structure – and value proposition – for different customer groups was going to be essential.

In January 2001 Dow Corning's chief executive Gary Anderson asked Don Sheets to determine whether and how the challenges the company faced could be tackled. The short answer: "By competing in the commodity silicone market and introducing silicone products to a broader cross-section of customers, including those who do not yet use silicones, such as organic chemi-

cals sector buyers." On the basis of the customer analysis, Sheets saw that the new commodity business could be pursued and Dow Corning's brand image as a high quality, high service silicone supplier could be protected.

There was no point in sacrificing one group at the expense of the others. Why dump an existing, profitable business model when you only need to create sales channels to meet the priorities of other newly identified segments? This is exactly what the XIAMETER brand is about and what lead to Dow Corning's two-brand strategy. Customers can buy from both brands – and many do – meaning they can take advantage of innovative products and customised services when they need to and simple market-based pricing on standard silicones when they don't.

Sheets also knew that being first in the market was paramount, so he gave himself one year from conception to rollout. The new web channel aimed to be able to handle first orders by the start of 2002.

Sheets' total development budget was a significant investment for Dow Corning financially. It covered hardware and software that linked with their SAP-based order entry-system embedded in a scalable high-performance IT-infrastructure. It included the creation of a new brand and all the branding elements including a new look and feel, colour, nomenclature, website, etc. Customer testing was also included.

But before he got started, he determined where efficiencies could be gained. "All the costs that were associated with our products and services were examined – mainly logistics costs such as warehousing, transportation, freight and customer service costs. We analysed everything through the lens of what we can get rid of. But you had simply to change the entire system to overcome this cost problem," he recalls.

The XIAMETER brand's client base could range from small entrepreneurs to multi-national corporations. Dow Corning knew from its research that all of them would adapt their behaviour and processes in order to take advantage of lower prices. So they all had to subscribe to one single set of rules, which were as follows.

xiameter.com from 2002–2009

Everybody would be treated equally on the platform, which would speak to customers only in English. Initial registration would be followed by a credit check with approval within three days. Shipping, payment and order processes would be highly standardised. For instance, a customer who failed to purchase with xiameter.com exclusively through its website faced a US$250 surcharge for having someone manually enter the order.

Driving towards an efficient business model, purchases had to be made in large volume quantities – tankers, full truckloads and/or full batches of material. This ensured no inventory on most products, which meant customers were required to give lead times of 7-10 days. A limited staff was put in place, significantly reducing the overhead required to manage the business. A small

Innovation Framework Enabling Module: Talent Management

The influx of new people into the organisation was crucial to circumvent the reluctance among existing staff to accept the new low-cost brand.

customer service and sales staff was available, but no technical service was offered.

To further improve efficiency and limit manual intervention, the business model was automated. When customers placed an order, it automatically scheduled production in SAP. Customers were automatically notified that orders had been received. They also received shipping notifications and invoices were automatically sent.

Credit terms were also limited. Standard terms were 30 days, however, customers could opt for 45- or 60-day terms at a surcharge or 15-day terms at a discount. If customers missed paying an invoice, their account was automatically blocked from taking additional orders. Only with manual intervention – and full payment – were accounts unblocked. This significantly improved accounts receivable.

At that time, customers decided for themselves whether this business model was right for them. Most products were offered through both the Dow Corning and XIAMETER brands so that customers had a choice as to how they wanted to purchase their standard silicone products. For those who could purchase in large volumes and truly wanted to buy at market prices, the XIAMETER brand was a great new offering.

All of this may sound strict, but, even though customers had been used to just the opposite treatment for 25 years, it was accepted because of the price reductions. The new channel took off in no time. "The XIAMETER business model paid back its investment in just three months. It is a lean, standardised process at lean, operational cost," says Sheets.

There was an important reason for building the new channel around a website and not off-line beyond the worldwide reach of the internet. "It is much easier to establish business rules for the customers and to enforce them if you have an automated interface like a website. Direct conversations with sales professionals only offer unwanted room for negotiations and exceptions," Sheets says. In his view the XIAMETER brand also created a mutual benefit in helping customers to save money. Customer staff is also freed up from running a sophisticated relationship with the supplier.

Yet a good deal of education, persuasion and gentle nudging has been necessary to sell the XIAMETER brand inside Dow Corning. The strict and decades-old science-based legacy had created a fiercely defended corporate identity. In many quarters of its business it was deemed just too risky to be innovative in a field that was not the company's prime area of expertise. In order to break that resistance early "…we had to move fast and we moved very fast. We did not have the time to get everybody on board," XIAMETER-chief Shelley Bausch says, stressing that setting up the XIAMETER team needed a lot of courage and backing from the boardroom.

Dow Corning took a radical approach in operating its new offspring. The XIAMETER core team consisted of less than 100 staff. "The only way this works is creating a team entirely separate from those supporting the Dow Corning brand," Sheets says. Getting the branding right was also decisive. The XIAMETER brand, which makes the claim, "silicones simplified," is operated as a separate business unit, but the brand is clearly endorsed by Dow Corning via the use of "from Dow Corning" in the logo. It was important that the XIAMETER brand not lose Dow Corning's brand recognition and reputation for high quality and reliable materials.

The XIAMETER brand had no direct competitors. Online marketplaces for bulk chemicals like Elemica or Chemplorer offer a full set of services and extras such as planning, forecasting, order management or negotiation facilities. "Our platform sold at a discount of approximately 15 percent in relation to Dow Corning's core products," Sheets says. Some industry analysts argued a two-tiered pricing system via two different brands would undermine the core business. Purchasers of premium-priced products – available for a lower price through the XIAMETER brand – would feel as if they were being overcharged through the Dow Corning brand. "The XIAMETER business model didn't cannibalise Dow Corning's business and margins because of our accurate customer segmentation," explains Shelley Bausch. So the real customer need appears to have been identified with precision.

The innovation's market success has been impressive. In 2000, Dow Corning had virtually zero online sales. By 2003 the percentage of combined Dow Corning and XIAMETER sales conducted online had risen to 30 percent – much higher than the industry average of 13 percent. In its first year alone the new business model reduced logistics costs by 60 percent, saving US$3.5 million, mainly due to more efficient shipping and the elimination of ware-

Innovation Process: Planning

The Dow Corning executives responsible for the creation of the XIAMETER business model navigated the critical planning phase of the innovation process adeptly. First, they made access to information about the project strictly need-to-know. This kept the project moving and minimised opposition. Additionally, they allowed enough time – 6 months – for the planning phase, and committed to a hard timeline with specific milestones for prototyping and testing.

Innovation Success Factors

Satisfaction of a true customer demand

Dow Corning successfully identified and segmented its customers' needs and developed two business models to satisfy them.

Presence of an innovator authority

At Dow Corning, Don Sheets was a critical driving force behind the innovation. The creation of the XIAMETER brand would not have been possible without his commitment and the commitment he secured from the Dow Corning C-suite.

Rigorous management of the business case

According to Sheets, the key to the XIAMETER brand's success was the understanding that cost savings were mainly in the automation of the customer interface, the establishment of business rules and customers' willingness to stick to those rules. During the whole project, revenues, costs and investments were accurately planned for and steered.

housing costs. The reduction in inventory, which is attributed to XIAMETER products being make-to-order, freed up further capital.

The platform also serves as a vehicle for geographic expansion. Initially selling in 50 countries, the portal is now configured to sell in over 90, some of which were even new to Dow Corning.

xiameter.com from 2009 to the present

After ten years in operation, the XIAMETER brand was relaunched with an expanded offering. xiameter.com now supplies over 2,100 products and still has no direct competitor.

Large volume orders have been reduced to much smaller, more efficient shipping units like full pallets. However, full truck or tanker loads are still available. Looking to buy just one bucket of silicone? Go see your local distributor. Want to cancel an order or change delivery dates? No problem, but it'll still cost you 5 percent of the order price. Need the stuff overnight? Fine, but please be aware of the 10 percent surcharge.

Some standard services like technical trouble shooting over the phone were also added to the model in the 2009 relaunch. Customers were no longer given a choice of purchasing from the Dow Corning or XIAMETER brands.

All standard silicones were moved into the XIAMETER brand and are no longer available under the Dow Corning brand – even if customers are willing to pay a bundled price.

And in a sign that this innovation drive is ongoing, the XIAMETER business model now includes distributors who can buy very easily and convey products through newly formed hubs, delivering further cost benefits. "In the beginning we had direct shipments to one distributor of around 65 locations in the US. Now we are shipping to only five locations, of which one location accounts for 80 percent of the volume," explains Bausch, who envisages the involvement of micro-communication services such as Twitter or an iPhone app giving xiameter.com even more reach.

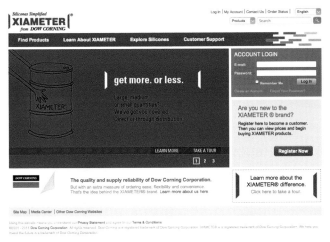

Source: www.xiameter.com

Siemens

07

Two old methods, one new innovation

Water is a matter of local pride all over the world, with regional tap water quality ascribed to everything from deep-rooted trees to alpine reservoirs. However, in many water consuming manufacturing sectors, hard science rather than geographical luck is what makes the difference when it comes to managing water quality standards, which are often prescribed by regulators. In this market, the industrial conglomerate Siemens, a leading provider of water treatment technology, found that rigorous product and process innovation helped it take on the challenge of a maturing market. By combining two existing water purification approaches, the German company not only injected significant new growth into one of its important product lines, but also met a clear customer need for more sustainable, small-scale water treatment products at lower cost.

Siemens RO/CEDI system

When it comes to industrial use, water is never simply water. Industrial plants often have a problem with varieties of water containing large quantities of metal, which corrode plant equipment and pipes or exceed environmental limits. Bottlers of soft drinks or breweries obviously need a different form and quality of H_2O compared to a pharmaceuticals developer, a metal finishing company, an electronic goods maker or a power generator. All these businesses have differing needs from tiny hamlets in rural Wisconsin with just a natural well and no access to a treated water mains grid. In all these cases, natural spring water, potentially full of unwanted residuals, is treated to make it either drinkable or suitable for various kinds of production standards.

Among the most commonly used purification techniques is a resin-based method using an adsorption mechanism with portable ion exchange (IX) vessels. Raw untreated water is pumped through tanks, pipes and containers filled with special synthetic resins – fine-pored substances that absorb molecules of unwanted residuals, eliminating, among many others, ions of chloride, bromide, copper, iron or organic carbons.

The tricky bit comes when the resin becomes fully saturated with ions. Up to now the purification tanks have had to be removed and regenerated frequently using strong acidic and caustic chemicals such as hydrochloric acid (HCl) and sodium hydroxide (NaOH). The significant disadvantage of using toxins like this has recently brought a rival process into use: ion exchange resins can also be brought back to working order through continuous electrodeionisation, or CEDI, a method that filters out ions by applying power to re-

---

About Siemens

Siemens AG (Berlin and Munich) is a global powerhouse in electronics and electrical engineering, operating in the industry, energy and healthcare sectors. For over 160 years, Siemens has stood for technological excellence, innovation, quality, reliability and internationalism. The company is the world's largest provider of environmental technologies, generating some €28 billion – more than one-third of its total revenue – from green products and solutions. In fiscal 2010, which ended on September 30, 2010, revenue totaled €76 billion and net income €4.1 billion. At the end of September 2010, Siemens had around 405,000 employees worldwide.

Siemens Water Technologies serves more than 90 percent of the Fortune 500 manufacturing companies, including approximately 100,000 industrial customers. Through high-purity water technology and related services, Siemens helps industry and manufacturers meet specific water quality requirements to ensure consistent processes and production. It also helps industry meet ever increasing industrial wastewater regulations, while improving efficiency and reducing waste disposal costs.

Siemens Water Technologies has 12 R&D locations and 151 people dedicated to research and development located throughout the world.

---

generate the resins. CEDI utilises no chemicals and creates no hazardous wastes.

In their innovation drive, Siemens' engineers spotted a gap in the market for a combination of both methods. The new device, created for smaller-scale water purification of around 8 gallons per minute, married RO with CEDI, yielding a whole string of cost advantages over the individual methods.

It was in 2006 when the German company realised that the market for portable deionisation systems – it makes up around 70 percent of the installations and about 10 percent of the value of the worldwide water treatment market – was no longer growing. It had even begun to shrink in Siemens' main market, North America. The reasons behind this were quickly analysed: on the one hand, increasing relocation of manufacturing plants using purified water to other countries, on the other, the emergence and adoption of alternative purification techniques based on membrane technology.

In order to tackle the problem, Siemens called for an innovation workshop. It was a broad gathering in which people from several departments – Siemens Water Technologies' "lab group," services, after-market products and research and development units – were pulled together to come up with ideas

Innovation Success Factors

Strictly continuous and open innovation process

The Siemens example shows how important a focused and streamlined innovation process really is. The companies' Research and Development Project Office supports the specific project teams, e.g. the RO-CEDI team, with a standardized Product Lifecycle Management (PLM) system. The PLM process structures the lifecycle into different stages, starting at the first idea, proceeding through development and market introduction and commercialisation. Standard milestones represent points at which project progress is assessed and stakeholders confirm the decision to proceed to the next stage.

Additionally, the project team addressed the interfaces between biology, chemistry, physics, electronics and manufacturing.

Optimised innovation lead time

This is an example of an innovation where speed was paramount. The short time between idea generation and commercialisation – it took less than two years – was essential in helping Siemens to fight back in its highly competitive, dynamic and shrinking market. The speed has already paid off. In North America the new product and service has already passed the threshold of profitability.

about how the company could get its market share growing again. "From the very beginning we committed the best people, people with very different but appropriate skills backgrounds. A lot of workshop participants brought a customer's perspective," says Andreas Hauser of Siemens Corporate Technology.

John Lombardo, SDI Product Manager, Light Industry Solutions at Siemens Water Technologies describes how the challenge was met: "In this workshop we discussed the key question of how we could grow in a highly competitive market with shrinking market shares. During our discussion we came up with the idea of integrating reverse osmosis and continuous electro-deionisation as a packaged product," he explains, going on to elaborate that the key innovation is the packaging of the unit, which results in a compact, skid mounted system with an integrated control panel and power supply. Several of the units can also be installed in parallel to provide higher flow rates.

But what lies at the technical heart of the 3-by-5-foot units? When the unit is connected to the customer's feed water source, the water enters a carbon pre-treatment vessel that removes chlorine, chloramine and other organics that could damage the RO and CEDI resin-based membranes. The water then flows into the RO housing where the bulk of the dissolved solids are removed. From there it enters the CEDI vessel, where it is "polished" to a purity level of 1μS/cm or greater. Unlike conventional technologies the new system maintains its high levels of purification throughout. "With the old system, the quality of the purified water fell significantly at the end of the device's lifecycle. With the new system we are able to deliver constantly high quality," says Andreas Hauser. As highly purified water cannot be stored for long, the system is also able to provide it instantaneously.

Most important, however, from a business point of view, unlike conventional deionisation procedures, CEDI technology helps to provide consistent high purity water without the need for regeneration chemicals or frequent changes of deionisation tanks. This reduces chemical discharge to the environment by a factor of six and the number of roundtrips from the supplier considerably. In addition to providing the CEDI technology, Siemens is able to bundle services with its offering such as maintenance and replacement of old tanks. The exhausted ion-saturated resins are regenerated at regional facilities and then reloaded into the vessels for future distribution. The customer is typically billed for each round of exchange.

The innovation significantly alters this business model. As around two thirds of the purification market uses small-scale treatment units, a disproportionate amount of the total cost goes into transport. Up to now, the vessels have needed to be moved between the regeneration plant and the customer site, often via distribution centres, by trained staff. Cost for transportation was also particularly sensitive to fuel prices and road congestion levels. In that regard, the new device reduces the water purification's carbon footprint considerably. The new system is sold to customers for a fixed monthly fee with no unplanned maintenance expense.

What's more, frequent visits to the site by the supplier's technicians can be inconvenient or disruptive for the customer, particularly if the site is, for instance, in the pharmaceuticals sector, in a sanitary or highly secured facility. These visits have now become obsolete. "You do not have to deliver 20 packages to customers every day. Our customers see us less often and our employees can focus on more value-add activities instead of routing the deliveries," John Lombardo says.

Siemens' new water treatment devices are already earning back the money invested in their development. "Speed to market was a key success factor for that. We went from the first brainstorming meeting to market launch in only 2 years," says John Lombardo. This, he thinks, would not have been possible without clear backup from an unwavering innovation authority pushing the new idea to market. "The commitment and involvement of management enabled the innovation," Andreas Hauser agrees.

Overall the new system comes at a lower price to customers who have no need anymore for direct capital investment. Since the commercial launch in 2009, over 50 of the systems, branded "IonRight," have been installed in a broad range of industries. The company is now looking to expand, selling the technology in other areas, e.g. Latin America, Asia Pacific and Europe. "With our level of installations in North America alone our investments for research and development have already paid back," says Andreas Hauser.

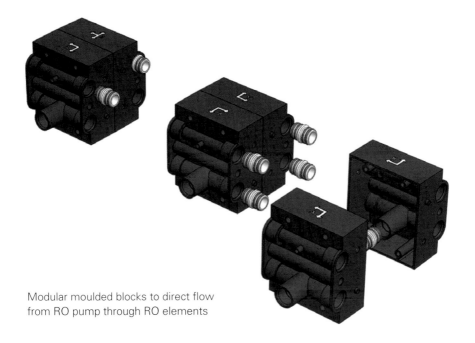

Modular moulded blocks to direct flow
from RO pump through RO elements

Perrier

08

Turning water into a winner

Legend has it that the Carthaginian commander Hannibal's pachyderm-backed troops, on their mission to conquer Rome, stopped in 218 BC near present-day Vergèze in southern France. Animals and men refreshed themselves at a natural spring renowned for its fine water. Much lauded throughout history, the crystal clear wells were finally also to be the source of one of the longest lasting marketing innovation drives in modern times: that of Perrier. The spring water's light carbonated fizz comes from the source and is not artificially added as it is in many other mineral waters. However, what has really been central to Perrier's 100 plus years of success as a premium brand is the vision of just two of its chief executives. As avid innovator authorities, they kept Perrier on track, imbuing a simple natural resource with a set of lifestyle propositions that have hardly changed over the product's long lifespan. To this day Perrier's brand power is well in excess of that of its peers, and shows no sign of abating.

Though he gave his name to the company, Perrier's founder was not one of its innovator leading lights. Louis Perrier was overseer of the Euzet-les-Bains spa operations when he first thought about commercialising the healthy spring water on a large scale. By day, he took the pulses of the *haute société* gathering at the exclusive health resort. By night he puzzled over how a cap could be constructed so as to seal a bottle of carbonated water safely for long shipping distances. The business-minded doctor even scribbled sketches of a green glass bottle.

In 1898, he finally jumped ship, shelving his medical career to buy a basic bottling plant for healthy water just outside Vergèze. Other small entrepreneurs had run similar operations for limited local delivery since the 18th century. Realistic blueprints and serious money for the business, however, only came to the table with Saint-John Harmsworth. Perrier met him by chance in 1903 while the doctor was struggling with his initial idea of selling spring water mixed with wine as an over-the-counter remedy to combat alcoholism in France. He soon leased and later simply sold the business he had hardly got off the ground to the Dublin-born entrepreneur.

When Harmsworth took over, he did away with the health proposition, being more interested simply in a normal soft drink. He was conscious, however, of the importance of visible "Frenchness" for his planned big-ticket water brand. That in mind, he kept Louis Perrier on as a technical director. More importantly, he chose the doctor's name for his core brand – a first building block for a product that, as yet, had no name whatsoever.

About Perrier

Perrier brand bottled mineral water is made from a naturally carbonated spring in Vergèze in the Gard département of France. St. John Harmsworth introduced Perrier in 1903, and convinced the British army in India of the product's unique qualities, which soon led to the brand's conquest of the other British colonies. In 1908, the plant was connected to the local railroad to facilitate shipping of the five million bottles produced annually. By 1933, production had risen to 19 million bottles, 10 million of which were slated for export. Perrier became the epitome of French *joie de vivre*. After World War II, another marketing genius, Gustave Leven, acquired the company. Leven promoted Perrier as the perfect tipple for Wall Street yuppies who wanted a clear head for their next banking deal. At the peak of its fame in 1989, Perrier sold 1.2 billion bottles. Nestlé took over Perrier in 1992, forming Nestlé Waters SA, which today leads the world bottled water market with 73 brands.

Contemporaries describe Harmsworth, who had no background in either science or marketing, as a man with the proverbial ants in his pants when it came to business ideas. Perhaps it was being the youngest of three children that gave him his hunger for success. In adult life his strong commercial instincts meant he was constantly bubbling with plans, strategies and ideas for innovative marketing approaches. "The mineral water, so Harmsworth thought, should, from the start, be positioned as a premium brand selling – at a premium price – something intangible, something like natural freshness," explains Emmanuel Manichon, Vice President of Marketing and Category Development at Nestlé Waters. Between 1903 and 1945 the product carried the perpetual tag line, "the champagne of table waters."

Under the new stewardship, Perrier finally took off. By 1905 Harmsworth had ramped up sales to 5 million bottles per annum and, in a further marketing coup, won "purveyor of excellence" status to the English crown.

Harmsworth harboured a strong affection for everything French. "All men have two countries – their own and France," he used to say. But the nation he admired, as he quickly realised, had centuries-old drinking habits that were difficult to reconcile with high-priced mineral water. In the cafés and bars of Paris, Marseilles and Lyon people drank mostly beer, wine and absinthe. Harmsworth's fine antenna for market development led him to decide that Perrier, although "made in France," should first make it big outside the country and conquer its homeland only later.

He was Anglo-Saxon enough to see the giant potential of a market like the British Commonwealth. Yet bringing Perrier straight to the mass-market of London's exquisite dinner parties would not be a guaranteed success, he knew, as France and Britain were fierce political rivals. So he identified the British military and its vast colonial spread as the thin end of a wedge he could use to push through his marketing drive. This had the potential, first, to globalise the brand quickly through the British Empire and then, thereby, to crack Britain's domestic market, finally bringing the healthy Vergèze water to the tables of Hampstead, Belgravia, Westminster and other affluent areas of the British capital.

With a highly focused marketing push, Harmsworth made sure that by 1910 Perrier had become more fashionable, fêted and talked about in Nairobi, Singapore or Delhi than in Paris. The higher ranks of the British colonial administration embraced the simple, somewhat outlandish looking French soft drink delivered in green glass bottles.

As Harmsworth had anticipated, the water went especially well with malts and gins enjoyed on the shaded terraces of ample colonial mansions in warm countries. "*Entente Cordiale* – Whiskey and Perrier," was one of the tailored claims for this target market. Another, referring to the same mixed drink, read: "Ask for a Whis-Per."

The mineral water established itself quickly as the perfect refreshment product for a lush lifestyle far from home – even if this lifestyle, with its scores of servants and stiffly elitist society gatherings, looked increasingly outdated. But an important milestone had been passed: the Perrier brand had attained a high level of exclusivity, successfully wooing affluent customers in a first pilot market. When Harmsworth eventually rolled Perrier out in Britain and later France he could therefore build on substantial existing brand power. It cer-

Whisper cocktail: Perrier and whiskey

tainly came in handy that his two older brothers, whom he had won over as media partners, were the founders of two of Britain's most widely read newspapers, the Daily Mail and the Daily Telegraph. This network considerably facilitated the British launch.

But as more and more modernity took hold in 1920s society life, a sporty edge was needed to reflect newly emerging themes of health and youthfulness. Ad designs and market research show that throughout the decade after the First World War Perrier was firmly associated with a vision of affluent gentlemen, not burdened by the need to work, playing endless sunlit tennis matches in plush surroundings while fashionable ladies watched, sipping faintly fizzy mineral water. This perfectly urban, as well as ultra-modern idyll of *savoir vivre* instantly struck a cord with the mass-market. By 1933 Perrier had approached sales of 20 million bottles a year, of which 10 million alone went to export. The close association with tennis was to hold for many decades. In the 1950s one advertisement read: "Au service de votre soif" (at the service of your thirst). Even as late as the 1990s, Perrier was a sponsor of the Paris Grand Slam tournament and of star players such as John McEnroe and Gabriela Sabatini.

Harmsworth, ever the restless innovator, regularly went to slightly esoteric gyms, where he was frequently subject to marketing inspirations while doing rhythmic gymnastics. As an outstanding marketing talent and classic owner-operator, he made the brand big for thirty years, more or less single-handedly. "All the activities Harmsworth initiated had a significant influence in clearly differentiating Perrier from the competition," says Manichon.

He cared about even the smallest details of the bottle design, which he felt should display exquisite, if subtle peculiarities. He decided to stick two labels on it, with a rounded one right below the top instead of the then standard square label stuck around the body of the bottle. The deep-green color of the glass had already been determined by Louis Perrier and has continued to be the recognised brand color to this day. But the bottle's form was thought out

Innovation Success Factor: Presence of an Innovator Authority

In this case we have two very powerful innovators: St. John Harmsworth in Perrier's early years and Gustave Leven after the Second World War until the 1990s. They developed economically successful ways to market sparkling bottled water. Both men had a clear vision about the future state of the brand and both used innovative new marketing and sales methods to successfully conquer markets – Harmsworth in the UK and France, Leven in the US. An excellent implemented growth strategy flanked by great advertisements and product placement positioned the nearly ubiquitous commodity as a fashionable beverage.

Gustave Leven

by Harmsworth: a drop shape, he reckoned – again suggesting freshness and clarity and something elemental – would make the product stand out visually.

When Harmsworth's era ended after the tumultuous Second World War years, Perrier's stewardship – as luck would have it – fell into similarly talented hands. In 1947 wealthy French businessman Gustave Leven bought the Vergèze plants including, the by now dangerously sagging brand. He was to prove another longstanding innovator, this one of 43 years standing. Being, in many ways, a St. John Harmsworth mark II – though much richer from the start – this energetic entrepreneur eventually turned the premium brand into the most recognised mineral water in the world, sold in 140 countries. He only resigned from hands-on management at Perrier in 1990, selling out to consumer goods giant Nestlé. By this time, 1.2 billion bottles of Perrier were being sold each year globally.

Leven had run businesses successfully before and already had a considerable fortune in the bank. He therefore saw Perrier almost as a sideline if not his pastime. This made him much less risk averse, which helped his brand building enormously. His key initiatives to lift Perrier to the very top of the market were more focused and sophisticated marketing pushes, the creation of a diverse soft-drink business around the brand and, finally, the all-important conquest of the US market.

Leven grasped Perrier's essential value immediately – not water but a modern lifestyle. When he came to Vergèze to negotiate his deal, he famously exclaimed, "Their raw material literally flows around their feet and they sell it at three times the price of milk or wine. This must be a good deal – I'll buy it!" On this former Parisian tradesman's watch the company, Source Perrier, was radically modernised, with new bottling facilities that could ramp up production steeply. By 1952 around 150 million Perrier bottles left Vergèze each year.

As the market for mineral waters started to seriously evolve, with strong competitors appearing on the scene, Leven saw that Perrier had to find a safe harbour. He aimed at reinvention on old foundations. A broader business for the whole company would give this plan a solid financial underpinning. He therefore built a small portfolio of water brands, buying budget rivals such as Contrex and launching new products such as Pschitt. These cash cows, he calculated, would support the core brand. He even had the courage to make the exquisite Perrier company the owner of something much more mundane: the rights to sell Pepsi Cola in France. Although aimed at the opposite end of the market, this was still a heavily lifestyle driven brand.

The Frenchman also poured enormous sums into buying the latest and sharpest advertising prowess available. Unusually at the time in Europe, he forged strong alliances with global agency networks such as Ogilvy and RSCG. Experts on the subject have dubbed Perrier's campaigning from this period one of the most spectacular ad pushes of the period. This helped it catch up with the way society's values had changed after the war. Greater social mobility and flattening of the class system was the emerging theme in many countries. "Against this backdrop, drinking Perrier shows its consumer to be well educated and part of the top of the social pyramid," says Emmanuel Manichon. However the core of Perrier's image – natural freshness – was sound. It just needed a more contemporary wrapping. What was essential, Leven said, was to redefine the mix of brand values the product was based on. "Taste,

Perrier in Vergèze

passion for elegance and fashion, joy and celebration, respect for others, humour and a pinch of madness," was his prescription to advertising professionals who scribbled the buzz words on their pads. Leven was keen to make it only a gentle re-brush rather than a full brand revamp. Perrier's perky ad claims such as "L'eau, l'air, la vie" (The water, the air, the life) or "L'eau qui fait 'pschitt'" (The water that goes "pschitt") expressed the new spirit: a swinging, uplifting, less serious and more vibrant element was added to the relatively static and almost aristocratically stiff image that had worked perfectly in the pre-war years. The sexy seventies were finally reflected in even more mischievous creations such as: "Perrier c'est fou!" (Perrier, that's crazy!)

In early 1976, the small green bottle at last headed across the Atlantic to conquer North America. "Leven did it against all the rest of the company. Nobody besides him believed in conquering the US market," remembers Manichon. Pundits at the time were of one mind in seeing Leven's plan as an exercise in hopelessly squandering money. He proved them all wrong. In 1988 Perrier sold 300 million bottles in the US – 80% of all imported water. Flavoured Perrier varieties were also launched there first, before their debuts in France. Conquering the domestic market through pilots abroad was, after all, the method St. John Harmsworth had used to put Perrier on the map in the first place.

The Innovation Process

From invention to market success

There is certainly no silver bullet when it comes to initiating and building a successful innovation process. Companies vary widely in structure, size, processes, legacy and culture, with so many nuanced dimensions at operational levels that there can be no uniformly applicable formula or just-add-water recipe. Nevertheless, there are some key general principles and rules of thumb that will be vital to the vast majority of enterprises in setting up their innovation processes successfully.

In Figure 1 you will find a compact synopsis of the innovation process. I will go on to analyse it in detail in this chapter. In addition to describing the six different stages in a proper innovation process, I will also isolate the relevant success factors. These will be vital ingredients for the process as they are overwhelmingly linked to management decisions and actions.

Step 1:
Idea generation

At the beginning of any innovation process is an idea. But not all ideas result in innovation. The early-stage visionary flash can serve as the basis for successful innovation only when it is conceived as an answer to an existing or assumed future customer demand. The crucial question is: how does one arrive at these types of ideas?

Certainly, creativity will not always be subject to detailed and reflecive planning. Archimedes, the Greek mathematician, had his eureka moment when he stepped into a bathtub and observed that the amount of water displaced corresponded exactly to his body volume. To this day, ideas with huge market potential often arise in a similar fashion.

However, they may also arise as the unexpected byproducts of searches for completely different solutions. In other words, it is a good idea simply to search, if one can do so with an open mind. A viable idea is often born when chance results align with already existing aims in an inventor's mind. Taking

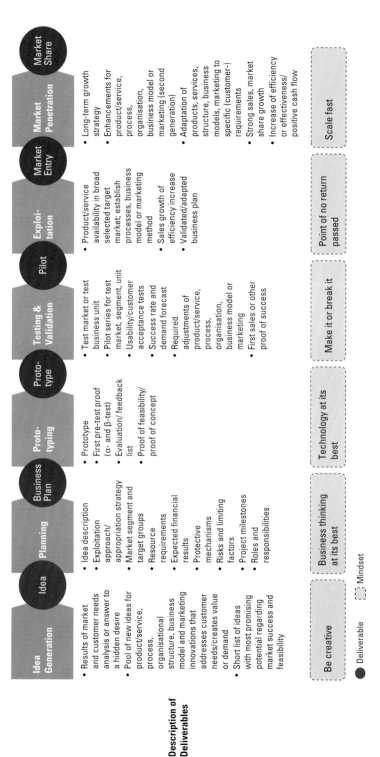

Description of Deliverables

Idea Generation	Planning	Prototyping	Testing & Validation	Exploitation	Market Penetration
• Results of market and customer needs analysis or answer to a hidden desire • Pool of new ideas for product/service, process, organisational structure, business model and marketing innovations that addresses customer needs/creates value or demand • Short list of ideas with most promising potential regarding market success and feasibility	• Idea description • Exploitation approach/appropriation strategy • Market segment and target groups • Resource requirements • Expected financial results • Protective mechanisms • Risks and limiting factors • Project milestones • Roles and responsibilities	• Prototype • First pre-test proof (α- and β-test) • Evaluation/feedback list • Proof of feasibility/proof of concept	• Test market or test business unit • Pilot series for test market, segment, unit • Usability/customer acceptance tests • Success rate and demand forecast • Required adjustments of product/service, process, organisation, business model or marketing • First sales or other proof of success	• Product/service availability in broad selected target market; establish processes, business model or marketing method • Sales growth of efficiency increase • Validated/adapted business plan	• Long-term growth strategy • Enhancements for product/service, process, organisation, business model or marketing (second generation) • Adaptation of products, services, structure, business models, marketing to specific (customer-) requirements • Strong sales, market share growth • Increase of efficiency or effectiveness/positive cash flow

Figure 1: Overview of the innovation process, running from idea generation to market penetration, with each step generating a specific result.

this fundamental fact on board, companies can do a lot to actively bring them-selves into idea generation mode.

A simple, focused technique is to collect and analyse information about what customers or users of a product think and say. In this book we profile the case of the oil company Marathon, a clear-cut example of this elementary-idea-generation method. Marathon's management asked its staff what they think an efficient "man down" alarm device should look like.

To capture information like this from customers and/or users, a company can create internet discussion platforms, allowing users to comment on each other's suggestions and sharpen ideas. This can be a rich seam for potential innovations. If wishes, suggestions and reactions can flow back and forth unhindered between market and producer, improved or even entirely new ideas for products and services can quickly see the light of the day.

Take the latest high-tech swim suits – or "body gloves" – designed for professional swimmers. They help foster muscular elasticity, boost heart ca-pacity, refine body tone and, because the suits are seamless and have special surface properties that reduce slowing wakes, give swimmers noticeably more traction in the water. Last but not least, the swimmers just feel faster in a high-tech suit, a factor that also improves performance. It's a terrific exam-ple of a product innovation that could not have come about without enormous amounts of input from users.

Companies keen to innovate can also create "idea laboratories" in order to steer idea generation. In brainstorming workshops, approved idea-finding techniques can be used to give birth to new inventions with promising pros-pects for commercial success. In these sessions participants are tasked with developing solutions for defined problems. To channel the finding process, basic rules are decreed that keep the exercise as creative, but also as target-ed, as possible.

A prime example of this kind of approach is the now legendary Top 100 Meetings, the creative gatherings Steve Jobs calls his staff to at Apple, from which the iPod MP3 player resulted.

It is advisable not to see the horizon of brilliant ideas as something demar-cated by a company's factory gates, but to embrace the concept of open in-novation. In the emerging multi-polar world, with centres of expertise scat-tered around the globe, it will be more and more common just to buy a viable idea from a rival, a start-up or an individual inventor somewhere "out there." In this new world, innovators will be able to tap into a rich pool of patents and trademarks as a universally traded commodity. Making maximum use of lim-ited funds also often creates the need to share innovation and its future return with external centres of excellence such as academia or research institutes. But a company's internal expertise can also often be complemented by exter-nal advice. A broad range of inspiration sources are also available at no cost: patent files, research reports, expert networks, databases and studies on markets and technologies.

However, the more sources a company taps for ideas, the more important it is to evaluate, weigh and critically analyse the material collected in an early

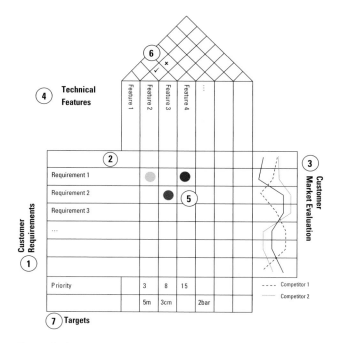

Description

- An easy-to-use graphical tool to compare customer requirements with technical features
- The correlation defines the best options of possible features in contrast to customer needs and how big the gap is that is to be closed

Approach

1. Identification of customer requirements
2. Ranking of requirements according to importance
3. Rating of competitor products by customer
4. Transfer of customer requirements into technical features
5. Set-up of correlation Matrix (requirements vs. features)
6. Define correlation between technical features
7. Aggregation of conclusions drawn in the matrix

Advantages

- Structured approach and thinking "that keeps you honest"
- Support though the whole innovation process from market research to product launch
- Helps to define product specifications
- Cross-functional team communication is simplified

Figure 2: House of Quality: transporting the voice of the customer into your business and facilitating cross-functional communication along the process.

phase of the innovation process. One has to be careful as ideas can have a magic attraction for their discoverers; the temptation is often strong to accept a false dawn. If ideas do not immediately display clear innovation potential – that is, the potential to convert invention into market success – they should right away be consigned to the freezer. In assessing this, it is all-important from the beginning that the customer need is the guiding light. Resources should only be dedicated where a clear need can be identified. Furthermore, the difference to already existing products and services must be as high as possible. Only a considerable degree of novelty will secure patent rights, so this is a palpable marker in judging an ideas's long-term commercial potential.

The House of Quality is a matrix conceptualised by Dr. Yoji Akao, who originally developed Quality Function Deployment (QFD) in Japan in 1966. It is so far probably the most useful tool for structuring the earliest phase of an innovation process – the creation of an idea. As a matrix-shaped planning mechanism, it is easily usable by teams of idea finders with no previous knowledge of the technique.

It serves as a basic exchange platform for reconciling ideas with customer needs. If, for example, the market asks for ecological or ethically sourced coffee variants, the steps needed to create the product profile can easily be extracted from such a matrix (Figure 2).

The end of step one, finding viable ideas, is a list of the most attractive ideas, each derived from concrete market demands and ranked according to expected commercial success and feasibility. Many ideas will probably have been weeded out by now, leaving a select few to be promoted to planning – the next stage of the innovation process.

Step 2:
Planning

Once an idea has reached the planning stage, the innovation process centers mainly around translating ideas into compelling commercial concepts, bringing them a step closer to market entry. During this phase, creative invention gives way to entrepreneurial thinking, critical calculations and sharp commercial analysis. A robust and exhaustive market analysis forms the central pillar on which can be built an all-encompassing evaluation of the project's economic and technical resources.

Fundamental questions have to be answered thoroughly. In particular: what is the core market for the envisaged innovation and how big is it? The end of this analysis is yet another round of consideration culminating in the second fundamental assessment: is the anticipated commercial success worth the investment? Only a resounding "Yes!" should promote the project to further stages.

What then follows is a phase of detailed standard planning procedures. Setting up a business plan now takes centre stage. Innovation projects become complex at this point. They now absorb enormous amounts of time, staff capacity and effort – but it all serves a vital purpose. Only a detailed business plan will ensure that everyone involved remains systematic and critical in the way they work and think. One of the big advantages of a business plan is that it provides a bird's eye view of the overall project. This can help resolve conflicts such as competing demands for funding if they arise. Detailed business plans are also extremely valuable as they can be used to measure exactly the state of commercial success once the innovation is brought to market.

As a practical guide, here is a list of the most important questions to ask during innovation planning:

- What market is relevant for the new product or service?
- What is driving this market?
- How large is the market and what trajectory will its demand side take?
- Which segments of the market or geographic areas are especially attractive?
- Which competitors are already present or are on the brink of entering the market? What is their expected market share once they have started?
- What kinds of products or services are already on offer? How does my customer proposition compare in terms of individual features and customer demand? How strong are my unique selling points in general?
- Are there barriers to entering the market? How high are they for competitors? Can patenting help to keep competitors at bay? Is the market regulated and if yes, how? Are there monopolies already established in this market?
- What protects my innovation effectively, and for how long? How tricky is it for competitors to catch up in technology and preparation for market entry?
- Do I have enough resources to enter and conquer the market swiftly? Are staff, funding and technological support levels sufficient? Can I secure a head start on the competition through economies of scale, steeper learning curves, superior experience and technology?
- What is the best way to cash in on the innovation return? Is it better to bet on selling directly or to involve franchisers? Is it preferable to give a product away for free if it will boost sales in other product groups?
- What risks are there in terms of unexpected bottlenecks or other restrictions? Can we master them internally through rearrangement of our processes? Should we enter an alliance with an outside partner to overcome issues of this kind?
- Also, how can we avoid falling victim to our own success?

Step 3:
Prototyping

So far, the innovative idea has been tested and evaluated on paper and possibly in computer simulations. The planning steps are now followed up by the first practical tests with prototypes. This is a phase chiefly concerned with probing technical feasibility – and it can often kill a seemingly good idea in its tracks.

How can customer needs and product specifications, hammered out in the planning phase, be molded into a physical prototype? At this point companies usually develop trial versions, physical models of a planned product, or digital models of the new service, process or software program. It is worth bearing in mind that, especially in classical product developments, this phase can require high expenditure as prototypes tend to be costly.

To keep spending in check, companies often resort to simplified model versions of an envisaged product, with reduced functionality. This is called "rapid prototyping" and is an established method in many sectors. Entirely virtual, computer-based trial versions can be created or computer-aided design programmes used to develop product models that can subsequently be transformed into physical models at a reasonable price using 3D printers. To ensure results will fulfill customer expectations, companies should have early alpha or beta versions of their products tested by trial users.

Prototyping is one of the most critical phases in any innovation process. At the end of this phase a decision must be made as to whether the project should go ahead or be stopped or altered in its approach. A lot of deep testing and intellectual evaluation work is involved at this stage and many additional insights, positive or negative, only come to light here. Hence the abrupt end of many potential innovations at this stage.

One of our case studies highlights the effort BP invested in developing its Ultimate Diesel fuel. It demonstrates compellingly what it means to prototype a physical product. The new fuel brand was first taken to internal test stands before a whole raft of external researchers kicked the tires on the claim that the petrol gave motorists more kilometres per litre while reducing both environmental impact and wear on the engine.

Step 4:
Testing and validation

Having survived the lab and prototyping stage and incorporated all required changes, an innovative idea has cleared one of the highest hurdles in the innovation process.

What follows is piloting, which means further practical tests, this time undertaken in live conditions. This is what will make the difference. For the first time, the new idea meets a predefined pilot market. The aim is to see whether it can live up to the requirements the manufacturer anticipated and also whether customers understand it and will demand it in sufficient numbers. To this end, market research is commissioned and detailed feedback from trial users is collected and analysed.

Initial sales figures, cost developments, and other factors provide information upon which a company can determine whether to proceed to mass commercialisation – or to scrap the concept altogether. It gives the project a final opportunity to be altered decisively if necessary.

Whereas with product and service innovations, pilot markets are outside the company, with process and organisational innovations, they are usually within it, with employees serving as trial customers.

Testing process innovations can often be tricky as companies need their systems, for instance the IT infrastructure, for day-to-day operations and frequently cannot afford to shut them down for testing. The test phase is therefore often skipped or shortened, with the new process being introduced right away. This is a risk that project managers involved in process and organisational innovations need to consider carefully.

Small and restricted trial phase markets are representative of the total market in which the innovation will be rolled out. Nevertheless, trial markets can vary in size considerably depending on how far the project has progressed when it reaches pilot stage. During this phase most companies focus on feedback from both trial users and experts. These are especially valuable in highly specialised industries. Software companies, for example, rely on professional feedback from external software experts during this phase as they are able to identify shortcomings more effectively than average users.

Step 5:
Exploitation

If testing and evaluation is a success, exploitation can begin. This is a decisive moment as the product or service is introduced to a real but select market. Only when this step is a success can the invention genuinely be considered an innovation. This stage also represents the critical point of no return.

Every problem that arises after this will only be reparable with great difficulty – as the example of the Mercedes A-Class model demonstrated. After launch, it was too late for Daimler to recall the car when it failed the "moose test" – that is, it tended to flip over on icy roads when swerving to avoid obstacles.

To successfully exploit an idea, a company can choose one of several paths. It can use the innovation itself, license it to third parties, sell it to another company, or make it freely available and generate sales via complementary products. An example of this last strategy is US software manufacturer Adobe. Since its inception, the company has distributed its Acrobat Reader software free of charge, thereby setting a universally accepted standard in the market. Sales are generated purely through product extensions.

To ensure swift and timely commercialisation, a company needs to ensure that milestones are reached and the rollout conducted strictly according to plan. Important goals in this phase are increasing sales and improving efficiency in production and delivery.

In order to monitor the innovation's market success, the company will also need rigorous project management that will constantly compare sales, cost and profits to the corresponding estimates before launch. Customer loyalty and satisfaction, the innovation's image and its impact on the company's overall profile need to be monitored.

A good example of best-practice commercialisation management was Gillette's Fusion Power razor, the first disposable razor with five blades and a supporting electric motor. Before rollout, Procter & Gamble identified the most appropriate sales channels and subsequently provided retailers with enough products to guarantee a fast and broad market impact. An aggressive marketing campaign via TV, radio, print media and the internet carried the news of this innovation to consumers.

Step 6:
Market penetration

The last step of the innovation process is focused on quickly gaining market coverage along a previously defined growth strategy. To be considered successful, this final step must deliver a substantial increase in market share and sales. Economies of scale and scope in production and distribution should start to reduce costs at this stage. As a rule of thumb, doubling the output of a service or product innovation reduces costs per unit by 20 to 30 percent. In parallel it is vital to further eliminate small, inessential product features and further standardise manufacturing processes.

When conquering new markets it is important to identify and react to ad hoc patterns of customer behavior and incorporate these developments into the medium-term growth strategy. The original product, doing well in one market, may need to be adapted for another. Launch processes, such as choosing the right distribution or media channel to reach the target group as effectively as possible, may also need adjustment.

At this stage, companies should also try to tap new customer segments. This enlarges the innovation's target group and opens up the opportunity for additional sales. An excellent example of this is the way British pharmaceutical giant GlaxoSmithKline succeeded in having its headache drug Sumatriptan – originally prescription-only – approved as over-the-counter medication, allowing Glaxo to expand its distribution network and attract many new customers.

Success Factors:
Making innovations last in the market place

Twenty years of professional experience in consulting has taught me that there are many innovation success factors (Figure 3). The more these vital elements are present and functional, the more likely the success of an innovation. This is also reflected in the success stories highlighted in this book.

Of the success factors listed, number 1 is paramount. If new products do not meet a real customer demand, they simply will not succeed. However, factors 2, 3 and 4 are almost equally important.

On the other hand, the chart illustrates that if individual success factors at the second or third level are missing or weak, other success factors can stand

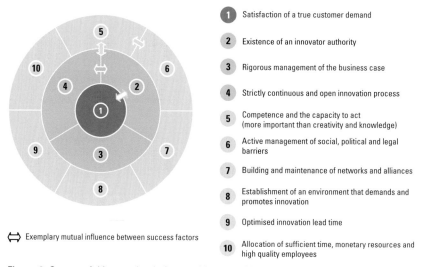

1 Satisfaction of a true customer demand

2 Existence of an innovator authority

3 Rigorous management of the business case

4 Strictly continuous and open innovation process

5 Competence and the capacity to act (more important than creativity and knowledge)

6 Active management of social, political and legal barriers

7 Building and maintenance of networks and alliances

8 Establishment of an environment that demands and promotes innovation

9 Optimised innovation lead time

10 Allocation of sufficient time, monetary resources and high quality employees

⇔ Exemplary mutual influence between success factors

Figure 3. Successful innovation is fostered by ten critical success factors that can mutually influence one another.

in and compensate for this absence to some extent. For instance, networks and alliances with external partners can work as innovation accelerators if the company alone lacks sufficient resources to develop a product.

Let's look in more detail at each of the success factors.

Success Factor 1:
Satisfaction of a true customer demand

Need is not the same as demand. Only when customers are able to afford a product or service does a need become a demand – and only then do ideas become innovations.

This can be strikingly illustrated. Take a look at Whole Foods Market, the ethical US retailer. As a result of the 2008 financial and economic crisis, the demand previously generated by health-conscious buyers of organic products was reduced to a mere customer need. Customers were still health-conscious and wanted organic products, but those products were now beyond their budget. After years of unstoppable growth, sales and profits at this high-end organic supermarket chain plummeted.

The opposite can also be observed. Bionade, a very successful German organic soft drink was initially introduced too early. At the beginning of the 1990s there was no market for organic soft drinks, so beverage manufacturers were not interested in this new type of thirst quencher. Only a few years later, German consumers started to "go green" and Bionade was perfectly positioned to satisfy a real customer demand.

In most cases companies are not condemned to wait until anticipated customer demand finally materialises. The example of Red Bull shows that demand can be stirred proactively. "There is no existing market for Red Bull," innovator Dietrich Mateschitz declared at the launch of his global market roll-out, "so, we will create one."

One of the main challenges lies in identifying "true" and often not very obvious customer demand. Henry Ford, the godfather of modern industrial process and product innovations, recognised this problem: "If I had asked my customers, they would have said, 'We want a faster horse.'" Ford realised the "true" demand behind this. He introduced the Tin Lizzy, the world's first car for the ordinary man in the street.

This is why extensive customer research, interviews and detailed interpretation of alleged demand patterns are paramount in the early phases of the innovation process. Of course they cannot entirely replace a good dose of entrepreneurial instinct. Even if trial customers confirm strong interest in a novelty, this by no means guarantees that the product or service will be a success in the market.

Market success will also inevitably attract copycats, but the more advanced a new product, the harder it will be to copy. A significant level of invention way beyond that of existing products allows for protection through patents for a period of time. Also, if the technology used in production of a novelty is difficult to replicate, it may offer additional protection. For service innovations, effective protection can take the form of trademark rights, unstoppable market leadership, being the quickest to market or a special entrepreneurial or cultural expertise, all of which are difficult to copy. In one of our case studies we show how BP's scientists put the greatest possible effort into creating a variant of diesel fuel that was truly new chemically. In another, xiameter.com shows that a clever business model innovation can exist for as much as ten years in the marketplace without attracting a single copycat.

Success Factor 2:
Presence of an innovator authority

It takes unusual assertiveness to engineer the breakthrough of a new idea. Many product, service or marketing innovations, as well as many organisational, process or business model innovations would never have come about had there not been a strong innovator personality standing behind them. For an idea to convert into a true innovation, there must be an authority who leads the entire process from idea to market success, a steely mind that never gives up and protects and promotes the innovation against all odds.

Some of these "innovation stars" are portrayed in this book – for instance Don Sheets at Dow Corning or Iberdrola's CEO Ignacio Sánchez Galán. They might not quite be at the level of an innovator legend like Henry Ford but they easily compete with outstanding innovators of our time like Sergei Brin and Larry Page, who revolutionised the global knowledge society with their search engine Google, or Steve Jobs, Apple's founder and CEO, the quintessential information technology innovator icon.

The latter also demonstrates how dangerously important one single innovator authority can sometimes become for a whole company in the eyes of the financial markets. "Steve Jobs will not appear at Apple trade fair Macworld in January 2009," read a statement released just before the fair, "Apple Vice President Philip Schiller will stand in for him." As soon as this was released, speculation around Jobs' health ran wild and Apple stock plummeted.

Similarly, it is also often unfortunate when retirement rules force a powerful innovator authority to give up their executive post at the age of sixty – standard practice in many multinational companies. In some of these cases a well filled pipeline of innovation projects abruptly stops being pushed to market and a costly innovation drive fails.

But it is not necessary for one single person to be responsible for innovation all along the process. It can be designed as a sort of relay. In the case of Red Bull, for instance, innovator Dietrich Mateschitz purchased the license for the energy drink from the Thailand-based Yoovidhya family before turning it into a worldwide success. It is at times tragic to see how inventors lose out on their brilliant brain children. The prestigious German Fraunhofer Institute, for instance, came up with the MP3 data format for digital music and video. Royalties for the invention still earn the think tank US$70 million per year. But the real commercial opportunities are harvested by the likes of Apple whose MP3 players rake up sales of US$1.7 billion annually.

Success Factor 3:
Rigorous management of the business case

As outlined earlier in the planning step of the innovation process, a detailed business case is an absolute must and the backbone for every innovation project. But this complex set of calculations and target settings is useless if it is not permanently, consistently and rigorously managed. The vast sets of quantitative and qualitative data that build its foundations need to be kept up-to-date, with new data integrated on an ongoing basis. The innovation must, for example, yield a calculated profit during each process stage, the only exception being the launch phase. If kept fresh, sharp and topical, a business plan works as a perfect early warning system over the whole process. A product that cannot be marketed profitably because the business case shows its technical realisation is too costly, or the customer target group too small, is no innovation. It has no chance of ever being successful on the market.

Aral, another of our case studies, demonstrates how well managed planning at all stages yields predictable results in the market. Identification of the right target market by means of a robust business plan was also a facilitator for Iberdrola's push into sustainable energy production.

Success Factor 4:
Strictly continuous and open innovation process

For successful exploitation, it is vital that projects with true potential are managed comprehensively and without interruption during each stage of the innovation process. Only a disciplined and consistent innovation process ensures that teething troubles are discovered and corrected well in advance of market entry.

The potential for severe brand damage is the reason why the innovation process includes a designated testing and validation phase during prototyping and piloting. Google is a good example. In order to detect and solve last-minute issues before product launch, the company provides beta versions of products to "early adopter and lead users."

Opening up the innovation process is indispensable as it allows the company to tap all sources of expertise available. Dissolve rigid internal structures and get people from different sides of the organisation – who might never even have met – to work with each other. This means, do away with "silos" – self-sufficient, inward-looking units with no great connectivity to the outside or other departments.

Opening up the process should also include suppliers, customers, research institutes and other partners. A particularly effective method of opening up is achieved by Merck. The German pharmaceutical company employs twelve scouts in seven countries, whose task is exclusively to make external knowledge available to it. In 2006 alone, these knowledge hunters scanned more than five thousand biotech companies and academic medical faculties. The yield was substantial: Merck acquired fifty licences and successfully marketed the products.

Another example is provided by the German conglomerate Evonik Industries. The company has instituted collaborative work environments – its Science-to-Business Centres – which unite all its research and development activities for a given discipline under one roof. The innovation process is not just on paper, but is brought to life in the architecture of the building and the set-up of the office space so that the employees can live and breathe innovation every day.

Success Factor 5:
Competence and the capacity to act (more important than creativity and knowledge)

To slightly paraphrase Thomas Edison's famous quote, we can say that innovation is one percent inspiration and ninety-nine percent transpiration. Leading-edge inventions are certainly a prerequisite of innovations. But experience shows that, more often than not, it is the innovator's implementation skills that determine market success. Take Aral Ultimate: the sophisticated manufacturing technology and the streamlined rollout process (following a company-wide standard called "launch in a box") ensured this product range's market success.

Success Factor 6:
Active management of societal, political and legal barriers

Cultural, political or legal barriers always exist in some form, though they differ from country to country. In Germany, for example, nuclear power plants can no longer be built as the government has decided to phase this technology out. There are, on the other hand, 60 new nuclear reactors under construction in China and 80 in India. Grudgingly, German engineering firms that were technological leaders in this field for decades have almost completely withdrawn from this profitable market in CO_2-free power generation.

The obvious lesson: to ignore what society as a whole, what politicians and lawmakers think, can be disastrous for a company and its innovation projects. Checking for potential obstacles on these fronts at the start of the innovation process is not enough. They require constant observation, anticipation and, as far as is possible, active management as innovations can only be introduced in alignment with society, never against it. Our detailed analysis of the specialist glass maker Schott shows how a growing trend in stricter environmental laws can be planned for and even capitalised upon through clever product development. The self-sufficient power producing devices Terra Power is working on – which we briefly touch on in an upcoming chapter – provide another striking example.

Success Factor 7:
Building and maintenance of networks and alliances

Nowadays a company can rarely implement innovations without partners, networks or alliances. Soon, pure in-house innovations will be the exception rather than the rule. This trend is clearly beneficial to companies as they no longer have to do everything themselves.

Networks and alliances often also open doors to complementary goods. A very aggressive and revolutionary approach in forging knowledge networks is used by Procter & Gamble. The US consumer products champion makes details about its research and innovation projects freely available on the internet, asking others – members of the public or experts – to contribute. This process is so fast that they don't worry about competitors getting wind of their ideas, as they believe they will be quickest to market anyway. This book's case study on Marathon shows how a close alliance between a company and external advisors can power an innovation – in this instance, a big leap forward in safety procedures.

Success Factor 8:
Establishment of an environment that demands and promotes innovation

Behavioral studies have shown that people are often subject to distorted perceptions. A sustained loss, for example, is felt more painfully than a missed chance for profit. Businesses should instead adhere to the motto, "Better to strike out twice than miss a chance to hit a home run." They should promote a risk-taking attitude combined with an entrepreneurial spirit among their employees. Only by accepting the possibility of error can businesses create a climate favourable to new ideas and projects.

It is also important to allot enough space and time for the company's creative minds to develop their ideas and projects. Businesses should promote innovative employees and present them as role models.

Success Factor 9: Optimised innovation lead time

In general, speed is paramount in innovation. As a rule of thumb, the shorter the time between idea and commercialisation, the higher the profit. Being first to market means that a company can firmly establish its brand as the pioneer, the original. This phenomenon is convincingly exemplified by Red Bull. To this day, none of its dozens of imitators have succeeded in wrestling significant market share from the archetypal energy drink.

The Spanish clothing retailer Zara excels at implementing this success factor. It not only has the shortest time to market among its peers, but also boasts the shortest time between idea-finding and positive cash flow from commercialisation.

So, if in doubt, companies should generally market a slightly immature product or service rather than run the risk of being second. Take the simple example of the video standard VHS. In the 1980s there were two competing video standards. The technically more sophisticated Betamax was unable to assert itself because its rival, VHS, was much faster in penetrating the market. Betamax eventually bit the dust.

The timing of market launch and the duration of the innovation process can and should be meticulously fine-tuned to optimise an innovation's market success. For each innovation, there is a window of opportunity, a period of time that is ideal for launch. One can argue that the art is knowing when the market is at a tipping point: ready but not yet too crowded by competitors.

Optimising time between idea and market does not necessarily always mean reducing it at all costs. In fact, only start-up businesses or companies launching products and services far off their core business and established brands should do this. Products and services aimed at a market where well established companies already have similar offerings must be close to 100% ready to go. This precaution might reduce market success but it also reduces the risk of irretrievable harm. A substandard new product marketed under an established, quality brand can have a devastating effect on the company's image. In a case study in this book we highlight xiameter.com, the new online arm of silicone maker Dow Corning. The case illustrates clearly how Dow managed to sell, as a lucrative sideline, its unmodified core products via a budget proposition with no additional services, without cannibalising its core business.

Under certain circumstances delaying the launch of an innovation, even if it has been successfully tested and could get the green light for commercialisation, is the thing to do. There is such a thing as launching too early. In the following chapter we touch on innovations in the making that still lack a clear route to commercial success. Among them is the smart grid. It is an intriguing case in which the idea is clear and focused, as is the business case. It is certain that smart grids will take over as the future of energy management, but it would be too soon to bet on any one of the many participants working towards this innovation as yet.

Success Factor 10:
Allocation of sufficient time, monetary resources and high quality employees

Spending a mere 1–2 percent of company revenue on research and development is too little – yet this is standard in many sectors today. Countless superb ideas have come to nothing due to insufficient resources.

The means companies must allocate for their most promising innovation projects are not limited to time and money. It is equally important that the most competent employees participate. No matter how much time, money, talent and leadership it takes, if this is what is required to launch the innovation successfully, they must be provided. Our case study on Evonik shows just how much support this success factor can provide. Through its organisational revamp, Evonik pours more funding into research and development than its peers and makes sure that their best people are allocated to the most relevant projects.

Innovations of the Future

Shaping our tomorrow

Let's leave the nitty-gritty of business analysis for the moment to take a swift and kaleidoscopic tour behind the scenes. Let's take a look at what's scribbled on the drawing boards of development engineers and the jotters of marketing managers around the globe and see what's being developed right now. Just in our area of focus, in the energy and natural resources sector, there are numerous ideas, promising intellectual progeny at various embryonic stages, awaiting delivery in a not too distant future. Some of them, from today's perspective, read like veritable sci-fi.

1. No more awkward entanglements

Imagine being a tired business traveller who arrives at the hotel room after a day of meetings and hard-fought negotiations, only to find your laptop and Blackberry batteries as exhausted as you are. This is where Fulton Innovation comes in. The US-based engineering company has pioneered electricity transmission without power leads. A hotel room fully fitted with their technology would allow you to simply put your laptop and mobile phone down on the desk and have it recharge automatically. No need to get your weighty charger out, unravel the knots and fiddle around finding the right international adapter before finally plugging it in. If this innovation project meets its goal, tripping over cables in offices and apartments will become a thing of the past.

Wireless power lines have an electromagnetic field between coils at their centre. The electronic device is placed between them. They are not new, but are not marketable in their current phase of development, since, currently, they only work well over distances of several centimetres. But they are already freely scalable between milli- and kilowatts, which makes them especially suitable for all sorts of charging purposes, from small consumer electronic devices to electric cars.

Early market entries by wireless products such as the eSpring water purifier, which totted up sales of over US$400 million, are promising. More advanced systems are in the test phase and can already bridge up to ten feet.

So, in the future we might easily see: workmen travelling from job to job throwing their power tools in the back of the van to be automatically recharged; whole houses functioning without power cords for toasters, hair dryers, TV sets or lighting systems; and electric cars you can recharge easily almost anywhere.

2. Prevention is better than cure

The energy and natural resources sector is, like no other industry, bursting with all sorts of moving parts. There are pumps, motors, rotors, turbines, drillers, blenders, blades, valves, conveyors, pistons and connecting rods running, roaring and rattling busily everywhere in the hyper-complex metabolisms of modern refineries, chemical manufacturing circuits, exploration platforms, power plants and paper mills.

The maintenance bill for the whole US manufacturing sector comes to US$200 billion a year and it is estimated that 33 percent of this is for unnecessary or badly carried out repairs. Furthermore, studies show that the average industrial company carries out most of its maintenance work in response to a problem.

This finding has created a whole new service industry delivering what is known as predictive (or pre-emptive) maintenance. It is constantly refining its methods, which, in a nutshell, consist in wiring up big industrial machines with sensors, continuously measuring vibrations, temperature, sound patterns, oil consistency and many other indicators of potential mechanical problems. The real-time data is processed by intelligent software that can, with the aid of statistical tools, predict exactly when a machine part is due to fail. The result is an extremely accurate replacement for all worn out parts ahead of malfunctioning, saving companies a substantial amount of money. The data is also increasingly used as evidence in court cases to prove bad practice in subcontracted maintenance, thereby further reducing costs.

This innovative monitoring procedure is already in widespread use by energy companies such as Reliant Energy, Enel, ConocoPhillips and Green Mountain Power and it is developing by the day.

3. Information is power saving

There is a sort of conversation to be had between utilities and their customers – but it's not currently happening. If somebody somewhere switches on a light in a kitchen, the local energy provider feels not even a tweak as a result of this marginally increased demand. All that will happens is the action will later be reflected cryptically on the customer's bill as part of an aggregate of kilowatts used that month.

Interactivity is virtually unknown in this sector. Neither energy users nor energy producers are aware of each other's behaviour and plans. The result is a huge waste of energy, but this is about to change dramatically in the new era of smart grids. Smart meters are designed to give utilities a real-time picture of individual electricity consumption down to flats and houses and then to individual appliances. The mantra will be: meter readings all the time, not just once a year.

The data will allow energy providers to counsel their customers competently about tailor-made pricing plans that encourage energy saving – for instance, during peak hours. At the other end, the meter displays will tell users how much energy each appliance or light bulb consumes. This will eventually bring both parties into step with one another and reduce the environmental impact of power production, primarily by diminishing peak demand and spreading it across the day to fit in with the most efficient generation patterns.

In the future such upgrades will be crucial in the big cities where most people now live. This is why the Dutch capital, Amsterdam, has decided to set more ambitious climate goals than the EU (20/20/20) and to make all municipal organisations climate-impact-neutral before 2015. One of the actions the city has taken to achieve this aggressive goal is the creation of a public-private partnership platform that will work with businesses, citizens and local governments to initiate innovative projects utilising smart meter technology.

4. Using the earth to stop the planet warming

CO_2, or carbon dioxide, is the gas most commonly implicated in global warming. The largest emitters are households, car traffic and power stations running on coal, oil or gas. One way of preventing CO_2 from building up in the atmosphere may be to capture and store it. In the developing climate change process, this could buy us time to research and develop carbon-free energy alternatives.

This future technology is getting off to a quick start. Vast reservoirs suitable for storage have been detected under the earth's surface and development projects are under way. The best storage areas are certain geological formations such as porous sandstone. This is why, for instance, just outside Berlin 60,000 tons of CO_2 will be permanently stored at a depth of 700 metres, sequestering emissions equivalent to those from 30,000 cars every year.

New horizons are opening up fast for this technology. Currently, CO_2 is being injected into a salt water reservoir under the North Sea, the first time this type of sequestration has been attempted. The deep ocean could, long-term, store further large quantities of the gas.

The development of power plants and storage facilities is also becoming interlinked. German energy producer RWE is currently one of the few companies worldwide developing the entire chain, from power generation to storage, on an industrial scale. But it is also now looking beyond this – to engage in microbiology, working with Brain, a leader in the field of synthetic biology and CO_2 conversion. The joint research project aims at an almost unbelievably ambitious goal: to create and scale processes in which microorganisms transform CO_2 either directly into biomass or into advanced materials such as bioplastics for the construction industry.

5. Nuclear goes compact

Travelling Wave Nuclear Reactors are a clever technology dreamed up by a team of world-class nuclear scientists. Under the umbrella title Terra Power, experts are piecing together a revolutionary form of power generation with the aim of securing the world's energy needs in the future.

The devices Terra Power is working on will produce energy for decades without the need for maintenance and are fuelled by waste uranium of low radioactivity. The nuclear plants we know today are huge, and need constant management and security surveillance due to the dangerous enriched fuel elements they use needing to be replaced every few years. The TWR technology, on the other hand, seems to promise the creation of much smaller customised reactors. They could be lowered deep into the earth's crust and produce electricity without requiring any attention for up to a hundred years. The devices, cooled with sodium, are fuelled only by a tiny initial load of enriched material. After that they will run on depleted radioactive waste for the rest of their long lives.

This favourable safety and sustainability profile has already attracted commercial manufacturers. The Japanese power plant maker Toshiba is running a pilot that is supposed to run for 30 years. Microsoft founder Bill Gates, one of the sponsors of the project, hopes himself to test a mini-TWR reactor for 20 years.

What is left to do to make this promising invention a real innovation? From a scientific point of view, just one thing: materials must be developed for reactor parts that can stand mechanical stress for the long lifespans envisaged. But, in general, the outlook is promising. Nuclear energy generation is about to regain favour against the backdrop of climate change, so TWR reactors should stand a good chance of success.

6. A desert harvest

Would you be surprised to hear that just one hour of sunlight hitting our planet delivers enough energy to power all we do on earth in a year? It is a scientific fact.

So how can we harvest this free energy source from space? Enter DESERTEC, a radically innovative network of solar-thermal energy plants designed to contribute substantially to the electricity needs of Europe, North Africa and the Middle East over the coming decades.

Concentrated solar thermal power (CSP) plants – one of the key planks of the DESERTEC concept – work like coal steam power plants, but with solar power used in place of coal. They will use a system of large mirrors in the deserts of countries like Morocco, Algeria or Saudi Arabia, reflecting and concentrating sunlight to heat water. The resulting steam will drive turbines for power generation.

CSP plants can supply energy on demand, as thermal energy can be stored easily with low losses. Additionally, at sites near the coast, sea water can be used to cool the steam power cycle and drinking water can be produced simultaneously.

A simple calculation makes clear how appealing this climate-neutral energy source is from an economic point of view. Electricity sent through the most modern transmission line technology from the desert would still suffer a loss of around 15 percent on its way from North Africa to, say, London. But the sunny regions chosen for the plants far outweigh that disadvantage by offering more than twice the intensity of solar radiation, compared even to Southern Europe. Studies have found that if just 0.3 percent of the desert areas of North Africa and the Middle East were covered with solar thermal plants, these area's growing electricity needs and Europe's could be met.

7. The smart way to put sugar in your tank

Transformation of sugarcane into ethanol is an area of expertise Brazil has been developing since the 1970s. Today's most active players in this field are Royal Dutch Shell and the Brazilian energy group Cosan. A proposed joint venture between the two, which still requires regulatory approval, would deliver 2 billion litres of ethanol per year.

The science is on the move, with a raft of new biomass fuels for the mass market about to become available on industrial scales. Given that vehicle fuels based on hydrocarbon – that is, crude oil – produce a third of all greenhouse gases, how can they be replaced with something sustainable that releases reduced levels of CO_2?

The latest generation of biofuels – known as fungible fuels – have to fulfill two criteria: they should have better energy content than ethanol and be deliverable through existing pipelines and tankers so that traditional oil companies can more easily integrate them into their existing distribution networks. Among cutting edge technologies designed to meet these needs, sugarcane-to-diesel is one of the most promising. Synthetic biology has come up with microbes able to transform the sugarcane's sharp-bladed leaves and stems into diesel fuel. Estimates put market prices for this radically new diesel somewhere between US$45–$75 per barrel.

Progress in this field is happening at breakneck speed. Building of commercial plants is due to start in 2011, with commissioning in 2013. As Henry Ford predicted in a 1925 interview: the petrol of the future will come from "… apples, weeds, sawdust – almost anything."

8. Stealth solar

It's time to lay to rest the endless debates between neighbours about whether they should be allowed to put solar panels on their roofs. Global specialist The Dow Chemical Company is about to bring to market a roof tile that looks like its conventional asphalt sibling, but is able to produce electricity from solar radiation. Covering your house with a photovoltaic roof will now be as easy as pie, with each tile's integrated circuitry snapping together through little wireless connectors. New shingles will go up twice as fast as conventional solar panels and cost about 15 percent less. Mimicking traditional roof tiles gives this invention a high probability of commercial success. Dow forecasts that their turnover will reach US$11 billion by 2020.

Dow avoided the blue shimmer of silicon-based solar cell technology by using a new formula involving a more cost-effective and durable PV material called CIGS (Copper Indium Gallium diSelenide), creating the appearance people are used to from ordinary rooftops. The new chemical composition also allows for thinner and more energy-efficient photovoltaic surfaces.

Dow has also covered the materials with a specially designed polymer that gives the tiles the same insulation properties against heat, water and snow as their traditional asphalt counterparts. This could be the start of a revolutionary photovoltaic dawn in roofing.

9. Oil from almost anything

The San Francisco based bio-technology company Solazyme, a leader in algal technology, has managed to make algae-based mass produced oil for fuels and chemicals, aviation, foods and the health and beauty industry. Now, in one of the most interesting biofuel development projects happening anywhere in the world, the US start-up has developed previously unseen expertise in identifying, screening and steering growth conditions for the aquatic organisms. Having worked out how to grow algae in the dark for the first time, the company will now be able to locate its facilities anywhere in the world, not just areas with large amounts of sunlight. It has also worked out ways of exploiting a wide variety of cellulosic and bio-waste materials.

The big advantage: where other biofuels require food crops, Solazyme's do not. Things like tree leaves, grass and chaff can be fermented, broken down into their basic components and fed to highly specialised algae to make oil that can be refined like conventional crude. In contrast to other industrial-scale technologies that typically rely on bacteria, yeasts or other microorganisms to transform feedstocks, Solazyme's algal strains achieve higher cell densities and productivity rates. There is also no need for change to existing refinery infrastructure or engine technology to handle the oil. This and the targeted retail price of between US$60-80 a barrel all points towards the new fuel's likely commercial success.

Energy and food application companies have already invested in Solazyme. The firm is also the only microbial fermentation company that has multiple contracts to deliver advanced biofuels to the US military.

10. Tapping into the warm heart of mother earth

Our Paleolithic ancestors climbed into geothermally warmed bathtubs and the Romans heated the odd villa with it, but only now is the massive amount of energy stored deep down in our planet – mainly left over from when the earth was formed – about to be tapped systematically to produce and sell electricity. About 10 gigawatts of power are already generated geothermally worldwide.

The US energy giant Chevron, running the biggest single geothermal business in the world, is at the technological forefront of this clean and almost climate-neutral technology. To take things further, the company, which first tapped geysers in California in the 1960s, has joined an audacious project. In remote Iceland, where earth warmth is more easily accessible than anywhere else, the most advanced geo-thermal plant to date will be built.

Drilling is underway on a 50 cm-wide hole that will reach a depth of 5000 metres. Water will be pumped down, then shoot up naturally through a second hole in the form of super critical steam, which is 375 °C. At a monstrous pressure level of 220 bar, the steam will then hit power turbine blades at the surface, generating 2000 megawatts.

The efficiency of this kind of power generation is tenfold compared to conventional plants. And this is only the start. Geothermal engineers have conceptualised drilling for a 15,000 metre project. This, however, would require a new exploration technology in which the drilling tip – enabled by electromagnetic forces– literally melts the rock on its way down to depths never previously reached while simultaneously lining the wall of the hole with a layer of metal. If this amazing geological endeavour turns out to be successful, the return will be massive: the steam hitting the turbines would reach an incredible 500 °C, making the plant even more efficient.

Conclusion: Eight Actions for Innovation

Exciting as they are, the success of all the ongoing innovation projects featured in the previous chapter is, by definition, uncertain. Only time will tell whether they achieve market success – the indispensable final ingredient for these brilliant ideas to become innovations.

Yet what is as certain as the sun rising in the east is how the innovation process of the future will look. In a truly globalised world, presumably around 15 years down the line, any investor will be able to set up shop very comfortably and easily virtually anywhere. All the necessary ingredients, from funding to staff to raw materials and knowledge will come through well organised markets at largely harmonised prices right to his/her doorstep. In such a world, effective innovation will be a question of survival. Certainly this will be the case for Western incumbents in the many industries with high labour costs.

Innovation is unique, inimitable, the punchiest and therefore most precious asset your company can mobilise. You'll know it's alive and kicking when your overall innovation strategy becomes your business strategy, when your innovation process becomes your business process and when your innovation culture becomes your business culture. Everything we have analysed in detail in this book's case studies shows this.

The approaches behind the various brilliant ideas these innovative companies have successfully brought to market can be condensed into eight actions of true innovation. Every executive who takes these axiomatic facts on board should be able to generate innovations for his or her company.

Eight actions for innovation

1. THE answer is: innovate

Innovation is the only possible answer for a company in the multi-polar world I have described. It is shareholder-friendly as it triggers internal growth and helps to replace risky and expensive takeover strategies. On a level globalised playing field, a good company will be distinguished from a bad one by its level of innovation.

2. Reorganise entire firm to produce innovation

To achieve innovations the entire company needs to be restructured and redirected towards bringing innovations to bear. Give your innovator authority, if it is not the CEO, as much freedom as possible. Then innovation will burst its chains and come to fruition.

3. Put innovation onto the board agenda

Where there is no backing from the CEO, there is no innovation, regardless of what other structures are in place in the company to try to develop new products and services.

4. Run company as portfolio of innovation projects

Companies need to run their business as a portfolio of innovations/innovation projects. Few innovation projects will survive, but the success of those that do will pay handsomely for the intellectual and financial effort put into the losers.

5. Leverage innovative experience to beat upstarts

A large, innovative company should, over time, be able to accumulate so much innovation experience that little upstart competitors will simply be unable to keep up. How can their modest means beat a big innovative corporation with lots of knowledge, skills and investment capacity? It simply isn't possible!

6. In big companies, ask "how" not "what"

For big enterprises the first question is always "how?" Ideas and hypothetical customer demand are always out there. "How" to bring new ideas to market should be your main concern. To ask "what" idea to come up with is the primary duty of upstart businesses.

7. Establish R&D equivalent for non-product innovations

Just as a department for research and development is commonplace in many would-be innovative product manufacturers, similar resources should be applied to finding new ways of running marketing, distribution, sales, services and processes.

8. Open up invention to the outside

Always look out for opportunities to open up your innovation process to the outside. In a multi-polar world it is quicker and less expensive to trade ideas and run innovation projects in alliances or back them up with knowledge networks.

The ball's in your court.

Index

About the Author

Dr. Stephan Scholtissek is Global Managing Director for Growth and Strategy in Accenture's global Resources Operating Group. A biochemist by education, he has been working on different innovation areas for the past 25 years and his expertise is now much sought after by those engaging in innovation and major transformation processes. He sits on several review committees for innovation prices and has been frequently published, most notably as the author of the Financial Times bestseller *New Outsourcing* (2004). His author publications are *Stromland* (2006), *Multipolare Welt* (2008) and *Die Magie der Innovation* (2009).

Crucially, as a citizen of Germany, Scholtissek's view of global business has been shaped by this former export champion, giving him an outlook significantly different from traditional Anglo-Saxon management theories.

Originally setting out to become a scientist, Scholtissek graduated with a PhD in biochemistry and was fascinated by the opportunities provided by modern science to combat issues such as famine and cancer through the use of novel knowledge and techniques.

West Germany's progress-skeptical zeitgeist in the 1980s, however, did not allow for German inventions in areas such as genetic engineering or molecular biology to be easily turned into economically successful products. Scholtissek therefore turned to business. He joined the medical technology company *Drägerwerk AG*, where, among other things, he invented a biochemical-based formaldehyde measuring sensor. However, Scholtissek's desire to contribute significantly to innovative products remained unfulfilled.

In 1997, he joined the global management consulting, technology services and outsourcing company Accenture. Here, he was able to work with clients and implement complete innovation processes successfully.